THE DELPHIC ORACLE

ITS EARLY HISTORY, INFLUENCE, AND FALL

THE DELPHIC ORACLE

ITS EARLY HISTORY
INFLUENCE AND FALL

BY

REV. T. DEMPSEY, M.A., B.D.

HEADMASTER, ST. JOSEPH'S COLLEGE, BALLINASLOE

WITH A PREFATORY NOTE

BY

R. S. CONWAY, Litt.D.

Hulme Professor of Latin in the University of Manchester; Sometime Fellow of Gonville and Caius College, Cambridge

BENJAMIN BLOM, INC.
Publishers New York 1972

First published by Blackwell,
Oxford, 1918
Reissued 1972 by
Benjamin Blom, Inc.
New York, N. Y. 10025

Library of Congress
Catalog Card Number 69-13234

Printed in the
United States of America

PREFATORY NOTE

ONE of my pleasantest duties in a recent term of office as Extern Examiner in Greek to the National University of Ireland was to read a Thesis on the *History of the Delphic Oracle* by the Rev. T. Dempsey, for which he was awarded the degree of M.A. with Honours by the unanimous vote of the Classical Examiners. The sound Greek scholarship and the sympathetic and temperate judgment which it showed, no less than the clearness of its arrangement, led me to advise Mr. Dempsey to undertake a thorough revision of his work with a view to its appearing as a book, and I am very glad to learn that this has been arranged. Though I can only speak with such knowledge of Greek Religion as comes to a student and lover of Greek Literature who has devoted some attention to the epigraphic records of ancient religion in Italy and in some parts of Hellas, I have found so much interest and profit in what Mr. Dempsey has written, that I venture to commend it to other students. I know no other treatise which covers the same ground and which presents the chief facts in so convenient, and, so far as I may judge, so trustworthy a form.

Prefatory Note

Readers of Greek history and poetry will certainly find in it valuable aid, and while Mr. Dempsey would not claim to have said the last word on many of the difficult problems which the subject presents, his work can hardly fail to attract fresh attention and careful study to an important chapter in the ethical, political, and religious history of mankind.

R. S. CONWAY.

MANCHESTER,
August, 1917.

vi

PREFACE

THE Oracle at Delphi is a subject of absorbing interest. Its long career lasting in historical times for more than a thousand years, with its origin lost in the twilight of antiquity; its wondrous power, at least in its better days, to sway the peoples of the ancient world; its constant intervention in matters of import not only for the state but for the individual; the strange phenomena of its inspiration,—these features have in all ages excited the keenest interest. Ample proof of this we have in the unflagging industry of excavators, who have literally stirred every stone on the site of the ancient Oracle, as well as in the vast mass of literature, ancient and modern, which has accumulated on the subject.

It may seem superfluous, then, to add yet more to the goodly pile. If apology be needed, I may plead, first, my deep personal interest in the subject, and, secondly, the fact that, notwithstanding all that has been written on Delphi, there is not in English, as far as I know, a monograph treating of the influence of the Oracle. The purpose of this treatise is to give a survey of the history of the Oracle as manifesting that influence.

Preface

I have dwelt at some length on the pre-Apolline cults of Delphi, and have endeavoured to show the transition from these vague, early cults to that of the clearly-defined, radiant god, Apollo,—most brilliant creation of the Greek religious imagination. The study of these early forms of worship at Delphi seems to me indispensable for the due appreciation and understanding of certain features in the Apolline ritual and mantic—aye, and for the understanding of the influence of the Oracle. For, the fact that the Apolline religion at Delphi gathered up in itself the olden sanctities of the shrine, and blended with its own traditions the legends of the older forms of worship, seems to have contributed in no small measure to the growth and spread of the prestige of the Apolline Oracle.

Next I have outlined the extraordinary influence which, notwithstanding some limitations, the Oracle wielded in well-nigh every sphere of activity, not only for the Greek but to a certain extent even for the Barbarian. The causes which produced such an influence, so alien to the Greek temperament, whose ideal was in all things local autonomy, the causes which broke down racial barriers, and established one great, central, irresponsible authority instead of the older and more congenial system of free divination, must have been very potent and far-reaching. These causes I have endeavoured to trace at some length. They fall under one broad classification : those extrinsic

Preface

and those intrinsic to the Apolline religion itself. Chief amongst them all must be assigned the creation at Delphi of an enthusiastic mantic, i.e. a system of divination in which the soul of the human medium is seized with a certain divine frenzy (μαντικὴ ἔνθεος, Plato, *Phaedr.* p. 244 в), and while under the influence of this divine *afflatus* shows itself endowed with a superhuman knowledge. This raises some very important questions—difficult indeed and obscure, yet fascinating for their very obscurity. The mantic ritual in vogue at Delphi; the varied and complex phenomena regarding the medium of inspiration; the nature and causes of the Pythian frenzy; above all, the question as to whether the Oracle was really genuine,—these are subjects involving problems which with our present data are very difficult to solve with any degree of certainty.

Having shown in a general way the nature and causes of the influence of the Oracle, I have traced that influence more explicitly in the three great domains of politics, religion and morality. In the sphere of politics the Oracle wielded an influence which is somewhat surprising to the modern world, accustomed as it is to see separation, if not overt hostility, between Church and State. The Delphic Oracle, though it failed to produce political unity, failed, too, conspicuously even as an adviser in the blackest hour of Hellas, was nevertheless productive of much good, particularly in the matter of coloniza-

Preface

tion. Of this Pythian Apollo was throughout the whole range of Greek history the guide (᾽Αρχηγέτης) and stimulus. In the domain of religion the influence of the Oracle, as might be expected, was most powerful. Failing, as it did, to effect political unity, it was amply successful in bringing about the ideal unity of religion. For, as Plato (*Rep.* p. 427 A) says, "Apollo of Delphi was the national expositor" in all great religious questions. A remarkable feature in the methods of the Oracle was the extent to which it fostered local custom and tradition (νόμος πόλεως, Xen. *Mem.* iv. 3, 16), not merely in political but also in religious matters.

Particularly interesting is the history of the influence of the Oracle in the domain of morality. Here there was a gradual ethical evolution from the old-time barbarous code which could sanction human sacrifice, and which took account merely of external morality, to the stage which took cognizance of mere acts of the will.

Having traced the influence of the Oracle under these three heads—politics, religion and morality—I have briefly indicated the causes which led to the decline of the Oracle, and have endeavoured to show the stages in the waning of its influence till its extinction in Christian times.

The subject is one of great interest : it is no less one of great difficulty, not merely for the amount of reading which it entails, but also for the obscurity of many problems which it involves.

Preface

When submitting my work for the degree of M.A.,
I did so with full consciousness of the task, so " full
of dangerous hazard," which I had undertaken, and
of the inadequacy of my performance of it. I had,
however, the keen gratification of receiving highly
commendatory and encouraging criticisms from two
independent critics of such standing in the world
of scholarship as Prof. R. S. Conway, of Manchester
University, and Prof. J. S. Phillimore, of Glasgow.
And in their verdict Prof. R. Knox McElderry, of
University College, Galway (under whose able and
sympathetic guidance I had studied), fully con-
curred. Acting on their suggestion I have revised
and enlarged the work with a view to publication ;
and Dr. Conway has done me the kindness of
writing a Prefatory Note—a favour which was
quite unexpected.

I wish to state here my indebtedness to one
work which has been of great utility in the composition of this book. I refer to the monumental
work of Dr. L. R. Farnell, " Cults of the Greek
States." His treatment of the Delphic Oracle
was naturally in so comprehensive a work somewhat
brief. In a few minor points I had occasion to
dissent from the opinion of so distinguished
an authority, yet I desire to express my general
indebtedness. Bouché-Leclercq's " Histoire de la
Divination dans l'Antiquité " was useful in many
respects. In reading his work, however, it strikes
one that less rhetoric and more demonstration

Preface

would be highly desirable. It is a matter of regret, of course, that the vast mass of Delphic inscriptions still awaits systematic publication. I have found, however, " Le Bulletin de Correspondance hellénique "—notably vols. xvi-xxi (1892–98), which embody the results of the French excavations at Delphi—of great utility.

I should not conclude without an expression of my sincere thanks to Prof. R. Knox McElderry for the unfailing kindness with which he has given me valuable aid in the preparation of this treatise, particularly by procuring for me materials which would otherwise have been inaccessible. I am also indebted to him for kindly reading the proof-sheets and suggesting many improvements.

T. Dempsey.

February, 1918.

BIBLIOGRAPHY

LIST OF THE PRINCIPAL ANCIENT AUTHORS
CONSULTED

Plutarch (with special reference to the Theosophical Essays " De Defectu Oraculorum," " De Pythiae Oraculis," " De E apud Delphos "), 10 vols. (Tauchnitz : Leipzig, 1829.)

Pausanias, " Description of Greece," ed. J. H. C. Schubart, 2 vols. (Teubner : Leipzig, 1875.)

——" Commentary," by J. G. Frazer. (Macmillan : London, 1898.)

" Homeric Hymns,"ed. Sikes and Allen. (Macmillan : London, 1904.)

Herodotus, ed. Blakesley, 2 vols. (Bell : London, 1900.)

——" Commentary," with Introd. and Apps. by W. W. How and J. Wells, 2 vols. (Oxford, 1912.)

Strabo, " Geographica," ed. Meineke, 3 vols. (Leipzig, 1866.)

Diodorus Siculus, ed. Vogel, 3 vols. (Leipzig, 1883–93.)

Pindar, ed. Sandys, Loeb Classical Library. (Heinemann : London, 1915.)

Sophocles, ed. R. C. Jebb, 7 vols. (Cambridge University Press : 1885–1907.)

Aeschylus. (Parker : Oxford, 1884.)

Euripides. (Parker : Oxford, 1897.)

Homer, " Iliad," ed. W. Leaf and M. A. Bayfield, 2 vols. (Macmillan : London, 1895–1911.)

——" Odyssey," ed. W. W. Merry, 2 vols. (Clarendon Press : Oxford, 1896–99.)

Hesiod, ed. A. Rzach. (Teubner : Leipzig, 1908.)

Aristophanes, ed. T. Bergk. (Teubner : Leipzig, 1857.)

Bibliography

Thucydides, ed. H. S. Jones (Libr. of Classical Writers). (Clarendon Press : Oxford, 1902.)

—— " Commentary," by B. Jowett. (Clarendon Press : Oxford, 1881.)

Plato, ed. G. Stallbaum, 8 vols. (Holze : Leipzig, 1850–71.)

Demosthenes, ed. G. Dindorf, 3 vols. (Teubner : Leipzig, 1856–61.)

Xenophon, ed. Zeunius and Schneider, 6 vols. (Leipzig, 1878–1906.)

Aelian, " Varia Historia," ed. R. Hercher. (Teubner : Leipzig, 1870.)

Lucian, ed. Jacobitz, 2 vols. (Leipzig, 1874.)

Athenaeus, ed. E. Kaibel, 3 vols. (Leipzig, 1887–90.)

Diogenes Laertius, " De Vitis Philosophorum," 2 vols. (Leipzig, 1833.)

Callimachus, " Hymns," ed. Wilamowitz-Moellendorf. (Berlin, 1907.)

Philostratus, " Apollonius of Tyana," ed. C. L. Kayser. (Teubner : Leipzig, 1870.)

—— " Trans., Essays and Notes," by J. S. Phillimore, 2 vols. (Clarendon Press : Oxford, 1912.)

Eusebius, " Praeparatio Evangelica," ed. G. Dindorf, 2 vols. (Leipzig, 1867.)

Livy, ed. Weissenborn, 5 vols. (Berlin, 1875–86.)

Cicero (with special reference to De Divinatione), ed. Müller. (Teubner : Leipzig, 1903.)

Vergil, ed. T. E. Page. (Macmillan : London, 1906.)

Horace, ed. Page, Palmer and Wilkins. (Macmillan : London, 1910.)

Pliny (Maior), " Natural History," ed. Mayhoff. (Teubner : Leipzig, 1892.)

Justin. (London, 1758.)

Ovid, ed. Burmann. (Amsterdam, 1727.)

Lucan, " Pharsalia," ed. Hosius. (Teubner : Leipzig, 1892.)

St. Augustine, " De Civitate Dei," ed. B. Dombart, 2 vols. (Teubner : Leipzig, 1905-9.)

Bibliography

LIST OF THE PRINCIPAL MODERN AUTHORS CONSULTED

L. R. Farnell, " Cults of the Greek States," 5 vols. (Clarendon Press: Oxford, 1896–1909.)

Bouché-Leclercq, " Histoire de la Divination dans l'Antiquité," 4 vols. (Paris, 1878–82.)

Foucart, " Mémoire sur les Ruines et l'Histoire de Delphes." (Paris, 1865.)

W. Ridgeway, " The Early Age of Greece," vol. i. (Cambridge Univ. Press, 1901.)

A. Mommsen, " Delphika." (Leipzig, 1878.)

J E. Harrison, " Prolegomena to Greek Religion." (Cambridge Univ. Press, 1908.)
"Themis." (Cambridge Univ. Press, 1912.)

A. J. Evans, " The Mycenaean Tree and Pillar Cult." (Macmillan : London, 1901.)

Th. Schreiber, " Apollon Pythoktonos." (Leipzig, 1879.)

R. M. Burrows, " The Discoveries in Crete and their Bearing on Ancient Civilisation. (London, 1907.)

W. R. Halliday, " Greek Divination." (Macmillan : London, 1913.)

A. Lang, " Homeric Hymns, Essays and Translation." (London, 1899.)

J. Burnet, " Greek Philosophy," pt. i. (Macmillan : London, 1914.)

F. W. H. Myers, " Essays." (Macmillan : London, 1911.)

J. P. Mahaffy, " Rambles and Studies in Greece." (Macmillan : London, 1907.)

K. O. Müller, " Dorians " (Trans., vols. i-ii). (Oxford, 1830.)

M. H. Swindler, " Cretan Elements in the Cults and Ritual of Apollo." (Bryn Mawr : Pennsylvania, 1913.)

J. F. Campbell, " The Celtic Dragon Myth." (Grant : Edinburgh, 1911.)

E. A. Freeman, " History of Federal Government in Greece and Italy " (ed. J. B. Bury). Chapter iii, " The Amphictyonic Council." (Macmillan : London, 1893.)

Grote, " History of Greece." (Dent, 1906.)

Bury, " History of Greece." (Macmillan : London, 1914.)

Baedeker, " Guide to Greece." (Leipzig, 1909.)

Bibliography

PERIODICALS, ETC., CONSULTED

" Bulletin de Correspondance hellénique," especially vols. xvi-xxii. (1892-98.)

" Comptes-Rendus de l'Académie des Inscriptions et Belles Lettres." (1914.)

Philologus, Band liii, Ergänzungsheft, " Die Delphischen Hymnen," Otto Crusius. (Göttingen, 1894.)

ENCYCLOPAEDIAS, LEXICONS, ETC., CONSULTED

Pauly-Wissowa, " Real-Encyclopädie," vol. ii, 1 (Apollon). (1895) ; vol. iv, 2 (Delphoi). (1901.)

Daremberg-Saglio, " Dictionnaire des Antiquités, Grecques et Romaines." (Paris, 1877.)

Smith's " Dictionary of Greek and Roman Antiquities," revised by Marindin and Wayte, 2 vols. (Murray : London, 1914.)

—— " Classical Dictionary," revised by Marindin. (Murray, London, 1909.)

EPIGRAPHY AND NUMISMATICS

" Corpus Inscriptionum Graecarum."

" Corpus Inscriptionum Atticarum."

" B. M. Catalogue of Greek Coins (Central Greece)," by B. V. Head, ed. R. S. Poole. (1884.)

LIST OF ABBREVIATIONS USED

B.C.H. = " Bulletin de Correspondance hellénique."

P.W. = Pauly-Wissowa, " Real-Encyclopädie."

C.I.G. = " Corpus Inscriptionum Graecarum."

C.I.A. = " Corpus Inscriptionum Atticarum."

C.R. = " Classical Review."

M.T.P.C. = " Mycenaean Tree and Pillar Cult," by A. J. Evans.

J.H.S. = " Journal of Hellenic Studies."

B.P.W. = " Berliner Philologische Wochenschrift."

Phil. = " Philologus."

Et. Mag. = " Etymologicum Magnum."

Anth. Pal. = " Anthologia Palatina."

CONTENTS

CHAPTER I

PRE-APOLLINE CULTS AT DELPHI

Contents

Contents

CHAPTER III

POLITICAL INFLUENCE OF THE DELPHIC ORACLE

Contents

CHAPTER IV

INFLUENCE OF THE DELPHIC ORACLE ON RELIGION

SECTION A: FUNCTION OF THE ORACLE IN RELIGION IN GENERAL

SECTION B: PYTHIAN APOLLO AS RELIGIOUS PROPAGANDIST

SECTION C: THE ORACLE AND HUMAN SACRIFICE

Contents

CHAPTER V

Contents

CHAPTER VI

THE DECLINE AND FALL OF THE DELPHIC ORACLE

SECTION A: TRANSITION STAGES IN THE DELPHIC INFLUENCE

SECTION B: ATTEMPTED REVIVAL OF THE DELPHIC ORACLE

APPENDIX A

THE PYTHON

Contents

APPENDIX B

THE HOSII

THE DELPHIC ORACLE

CHAPTER I

PRE-APOLLINE CULTS OF DELPHI

Introduction

Πρῶτον μὲν εὐχῇ τῆδε πρεσβεύω θεῶν
τὴν πρωτόμαντιν Γαῖαν· ἐκ δὲ τῆς Θέμιν,
ἣ δὴ τὸ μητρὸς δευτέρα τόδ' ἕζετο
μαντεῖον, ὡς λόγος τις· ἐν δὲ τῷ τρίτῳ
λάχει, θελούσης, οὐδὲ πρὸς βίαν τινὸς,
Τιτανὶς ἄλλη παῖς χθονὸς καθέζετο
Φοίβη· δίδωσι δ' ἣ γενέθλιον δόσιν
Φοίβῳ. κ.τ.λ.—AESCH. Eum. I ff.

WHEN we think of the Delphic Oracle, at once the image of the golden-haired Apollo, " lord of the silver bow," ideal of grace and strength and dignity, comes up before our minds. Yet Delphi, or, as it was anciently called, Pytho,[1] was not always

[1] We may take it that the name Pytho is anterior to that of Delphi. Pytho (Πυθώ) alone is known to Homer (vid. Il. ii. 519 Πυθῶνά τε πετρηέσσαν, ix. 405 Πυθοῖ ἔνι πετρηέσσῃ ; Od. viii. 80 Πυθοῖ ἐν ἠγαθέῃ, cf. Hes. Th. 499, etc.), while the name Delphi (Δελφοί) is found for the first time in the Homeridae. Vid. Hom. Hymn. Dian. (xxvii. in Sikes and Allen), 14. Cf. the fragment of Heraclitus quoted

I

The Delphic Oracle

sacred to the brightest of the bright Olympians :
it knew of older and darker cults before the North-
erns [1] planted the Apolline worship at the foot of

by Plut. De Pyth. Orac. xxi. According to *P.W.* (s.v.
Delphoi, 2526), the vernacular form of Δελφοί till about the
middle of the 4th cent. B.C. was Δαλφοί. This is proved by
coinage. Vid. " B. M. Catalogue of Greek Coins " (B. V. Head,
ed. Poole), pp. xxxi, 26. A noteworthy difference between the
names is that, while Pytho was used to designate both the city
itself and the part of Phocis which lay round the foot of Parnassus, Delphi never designated anything but the city itself.
Vid. Liddell and Scott, Lexicon, s.v. Πυθώ. As to the meaning
and derivation of these names, there are manifold theories—
some of them highly fanciful—ancient and modern. Vid.
(among ancient authors) Hom. Hymn. Ap. 372 ; Strab., 419
κεκλῆσθαι . . . καὶ τὴν πόλιν ἀπὸ τοῦ πυθέσθαι, acc. to which
derivation Πυθώ would simply be the " place of inquiry " (cf.
Soph. O.T. 603–4, Πυθώ δ' ἰὼν | πεύθευ τὰ χρησθέντ᾽) ; Paus.
x. 6. 5. The last-mentioned writer shows that the common
explanation in ancient times was that given by the writer of
the Hom. Hymn. Ap. 372, namely that Πυθώ was derived
from πύθεσθαι, "rot," because the dragon slain by Apollo
there rotted. Cf. Hom. Hymn. Ap. 363, ἐνταυθοῖ νῦν πύθευ ἐπὶ
χθονὶ βωτιανείρῃ.

Among modern authors vid. Bouché-Leclercq, " La Div.
dans l'Antiq." pp. 51, 64 ; *P.W.* s.v. Delphoi (Hiller von Gaertringen), 2525–6 ; ibid. s.v. Apollon (Wernicke), 5 ; Sikes
and Allen, Hom. Hymn. Ap. 372 note ; A. Mommsen, "Delphika," p. 13. It seems safest to accept the etymology of the
writer of the Hom. Hymn—that Πυθώ comes from πύθεσθαι,
" rot," the reference being probably to some physical peculiarity of the place, either to foul-smelling vapours, or else
possibly to a property of the stones there which have a tendency
to scale off. A. Mommsen, " Delphika," p. 13, with whom the
writer (H. von Gaertringen) in *P.W.* (s.v. Delphoi), 2525, agrees,
compares Faulhorn in the Bernese Alps.

[1] In the much-vexed question of the original home of Apollo
—which seems impossible to fix with certainty according to

Pre-Apolline Cults of Delphi

snow-crowned Parnassus. The nature of these cults we shall presently consider. Their study is of the highest importance, as it helps us to understand many traits in the Apolline ritual and mantic, which would otherwise be inexplicable. Furthermore, as we shall see, they contributed in no small measure to the subsequent growth of the influence of the Oracle.

Section A : Ge

The early history of the Delphic Oracle is in the main clear enough, though indeed at times it is none too easy to unweave the tissue of myth and legend which Greek religious fancy has woven round its central shrine. The order of the different cults, as given by the various mythographers, is substantially the same.[1] Consequently we have no reason to doubt that it corresponds with some historical reality. We may accept the unanimous testimony of antiquity—testimony given in the very hey-day of Apolline glory—that Ge (Gaea), the Earth-goddess, was the original possessor. Thus in Aes-

present data—I follow as the most probable the conclusion of Farnell, " Cults of the Greek States," iv. p. 99 ff. For a summary of the manifold views on the subject—without, however, a criticism of any view—vid. a monograph by M. H. Swindler, " Cretan Elements in the Cult and Ritual of Apollo" (Bryn Mawr, Penn. 1913), p. 11 ff.

[1] Cf. Bouché-Leclercq, " La Div. dans l'Antiq." iii. p. 46 and note.

The Delphic Oracle

chylus [1] the Pythia, or priestess of Apollo, in her opening prayer, first invokes " Gaea, the primal prophetess." Pausanias [2] says that " in the most ancient times the oracle was an oracle of Earth." Plutarch,[3] and Diodorus Siculus [4] make similar statements. Certainly that the Earth-goddess was once a Delphic divinity is borne out by evidences archaeological, literary and ritual. A recently-discovered inscription speaks of a temple of Ge at Delphi,[5] and Plutarch tells us that her temple at Delphi stood on the south of Apollo's,[6] near the water of Castalia.[7] Perhaps Mnaseas of Patrae [8]

[1] Eum. 2, τὴν πρωτόμαντιν Γαῖαν.

[2] x. 5. 5, φασὶ γὰρ δὴ τὰ ἀρχαιότατα Γῆς εἶναι τὸ χρηστήριον.

[3] De Pyth. Orac. xvii.

[4] xvi. 26. 4.   [5] τὸ Γᾶς ἱερόν, vid. B.C.H. xvi. p. 65.

[6] It is interesting to note that in Irish mythology Earth, under the name of Tailtiu, is frequently associated with the solar god, Lug (= Gaulish Lugu-s, whence Lugu-dunum), being usually represented as his nursing mother. Cf. M. Jules Loth in "Comptes Rendus," 1914, p. 189.

[7] De Pyth. Orac. xvii. ; cf. B.C.H. xvii. p. 619. Between the Treasury of the Athenians and the Portico to the north of the Sacred Way, the French excavators found a pool in connexion with an aqueduct, plunging under the temple, which is certainly the ἀναπνοή of Plutarch. Here, then, must have been the sanctuary of Earth and the Muses mentioned by Plut. (ibid.). There also must have been the primitive oracle of which Earth and Themis were the mistresses, and of which Python was the guardian. The grotto concealed the dragon. Cf. Foucart, " Mém. sur Delph." pp. 94–5.

[8] Vid. Farnell, " Cults," iii. p. 308. Certainly the epithet " the broad-bosomed one " (Εὐρύστερνος) seems a most appropriate one for the Earth-goddess. Cf. Γαῖ' εὐρύστερνος, Hes. Th. 117.

refers to this also, when in his collection of Delphic responses he mentions " the temple of the broad-bosomed one." The Naxians erected in honour of the Earth-oracle at Delphi a colossal sphinx. They set it up in the precinct of Ge, and traces of it have been found in the recent French excavations.[1]

The Earth-goddess's early connexion with Delphi is also shown by certain features in the ritual of later Delphic divination. The Pythia's inspiration drawn from subterranean sources : her drinking of the sacred spring preparatory to oracular utter-ance,[2] her receiving through a cleft in the earth a vapour producing (according to many writers) a prophetic trance[3]—such divination is surely chthonian, belonging to an older stratum of religion. Why should the bright, genial god, Apollo, resort to the dark mantic methods of the nether powers? Finally, the famous story of Apollo's struggle at Delphi against the Python,[4] " child of Earth," and guardian of her shrine, proves Earth's early asso-ciations with the Oracle.

Here we may ask the question, Why was Ge mantic ? The answer seems to be that, as the earth was the abode of the dead, consequently the

[1] Vid. Miss Harrison, " Prolegomena," p. 210, quoting from Homolle, " Fouilles de Delphes," 1902, pl. xiv.

[2] For a discussion of the mantic ritual at Delphi vid. infr. p. 49 ff.

[3] Vid. infr. p. 57 ff.

[4] For relations of the Python with Earth vid. infr. pp. 157–61 and App. A.

The Delphic Oracle

Earth-divinity controlled the realm of spirits, which were regarded as endowed with prophetic powers. That the spirits of the dead were believed to possess such powers is proved, in the first place, by hero-worship—for heroes sometimes had oracular shrines [1]—and secondly, by necromancy, that is, the evocation of spirits of the dead for mantic purposes (νέκυια). This practice was frequently resorted to in antiquity,[2] and apparently it has its modern counterpart in Spiritism, which professes to evolve a new creed from so-called Spirit-revelation.[3] Again, dreams, which often foreshadowed the future, were supposed to ascend

[1] The most famous was that of Trophonius at Lebadea (modern Livadia) in Boeotia. For a full account of this oracle vid. Pausanias (who had himself consulted it), ix. 39. Cf. Bouché-Leclercq, "La Div." iii. pp. 321–32. Amphiaraus had oracles at Thebes and Oropus, vid. Hdt. i. 46, viii. 134; Paus. i. 34. 5. Cf. Bouché-Leclercq, ibid. pp. 334–7. Tiresias had an oracle at Orchomenus, vid. Plut. De Def. Orac. xliv. Cf. Bouché-Leclercq, ibid. p. 333.

[2] Vid. Od. xi. 36–37 (indeed the whole of Od. xi. is commonly called Νέκυια); Aesch. Pers. 681 ff. where the ghost of Darius is evoked. Cf. 1 Samuel xxviii. (where the witch of Endor summons up the ghost of Samuel at the instance of Saul), and numerous condemnations of Spiritistic practices in O.T. e.g. Lev. xx. 6, 27; Deut. xviii. 9–12, etc.

[3] Spiritism, though condemned by all churches, because of its dangers, is widely diffused at present. For literature on the subject vid. Lapponi, " Hypnotism and Spiritism "; McKenzie, " Spirit Intercourse," a book containing some amazing—and indeed amusing—statements; Hudson, " Psychic Phenomena "; A. V. Miller, " Sermons on Modern Spiritualism "; Raupert, " Dangers of Spiritualism "; Barrett, " Psychical Research."

Pre-Apolline Cults of Delphi

from the world below.[1] Consequently, the Earth-divinity might acquire oracular functions exercised especially through the process of "incubation" (ἐγκοίμησις),[2] in which the consultant slept in the

[1] Cf. Eur. I.T. 1260 ff.

> νύχια
> χθὼν ἐτεκνώσατο φάσματ' ὀνείρων,
> οἳ πόλεσι μερόπων κ.τ.λ.

That dreams came from the world below is clear also from the "incubation" ritual.

[2] For the word vid. Diod. i. 53. This ἐγκοίμησις (Lat. *incubatio*), or sleeping in the shrine, was an essential part of Asclepius's healing ritual, the cure being given or revealed in a dream. Cf. Ar. Plut. 411–12, κατακλίνειν αὐτὸν εἰς Ἀσκληπίου; Pl. Curc. I. i. 61: "hic leno aegrotus incubat in Aesculapii fano"; Cic. De Div. ii. 59, § 123, "an Aesculapius, an Serapis potest nobis praescribere per somnium curationem valetudinis, etc.?" For this method of divination vid. Bouché-Leclercq, op. cit. iii. p. 286; Myers, "Essays," p. 16.

The dream-oracle was specially associated with heroes and the chthonian powers. For the dream-oracle of Amphiaraus vid. Paus. i. 34. 5. Here we are told that consultants used to sacrifice a ram, on whose skin they slept and awaited a revelation in a dream. This ritual reminds us of the Διὸς κῴδιον, the magic fleece used in the propitiatory ceremonies of Zeus Meilichios, and also at the Eleusinian mysteries (vid. Suidas, i. 1, p. 1404, quoted by Farnell, op. cit. i. p. 172). Halliday, "Greek Divination," p. 128 ff., points out an interesting ancient Gaelic parallel. In the rite known as Taghairm (probably meaning "echo") the consultant was wrapped in a cow-hide and left beside a spring during the night where he obtained inspiration from visions. For oneiromancy, or divination from dreams, in general vid. Cic. De Div. i. 20 ff., ii. 58 ff. He regards oracles from dreams, like those from inspired frenzy, as belonging to natural divination. Both methods, according to Cratippus, whom he quotes (i. 32, § 70), are to be explained by the supposition that the soul, whether

The Delphic Oracle

shrine with his ear upon the ground. Thus, too, we should explain the tradition that Night (*Νύξ*) was sometimes thought to take the place of Earth at the Oracle of Delphi [1] : Earth and Night were both mothers of dreams.[2]

How came the Earth-goddess to have a shrine at Delphi ? Certainly there must have been some special physical features, apart from mere natural impressiveness, which marked out the place for mantic purposes as a shrine of Ge. But what exactly these features were it is difficult to say with certainty. The current local tradition of the discovery of the Oracle is this. In the place afterwards occupied by the *adytum*, or innermost shrine of the sanctuary, there was a chasm in the ground. Delphi being as yet uninhabited, a flock of goats was browsing near the chasm, and each goat as it approached the chasm and looked into it began to skip about and utter unwonted sounds. The goat-

dreaming or actuated by divine frenzy, is partially rapt out of the body, the powers of the rational part of the soul being greater in proportion as they are untrammelled by the irrational element. For a treatment of the question of oneiromancy by modern authors vid. Bouché-Leclercq, op. cit. i. ; Myers, " Essays," p. 16.

[1] Vid. Schol. Pind. P. Argum. εἶτα ἔρχεται (sc. ὁ Ἀπόλλων) ἐπὶ τὸ μαντεῖον, ἐν ᾧ πρώτη Νύξ ἐχρησμῴδησεν, εἶτα Θέμις. Cf. Plut. De Ser. Num. Vind. xxii. where it is said that Night was thought by some to share with Apollo the oracle at Delphi. . . . ὡς κοινὸν εἴη μαντεῖον ἐν Δελφοῖς Ἀπόλλωνος καὶ Νυκτός.

[2] Cf. Eur. I.T. 1263; Hec. 70-1 ; Plut. De Ser. Num. Vind. xxii.

8

herd wondered at the strange phenomenon, and approaching the chasm had the same experience as his goats, and forthwith began to prophesy. The fame of this went abroad, and many visited the place, all experiencing a like prophetic ecstasy. So the place was considered the oracular shrine of Earth. Afterwards as many in their prophetic frenzy jumped into the chasm and disappeared, the dwellers round the place determined, in order to obviate the danger, to appoint one woman as prophetess. And in order that she might receive the prophetic influence and give the oracles in safety they devised a three-legged machine or tripod, which she mounted when about to prophesy.[1] According to Plutarch,[2] the shepherd who first discovered the inspiring influence of the cavern was Coretas.[3]

Such is the traditional account of the founding of the Earth-oracle at Delphi—an account which is merely aetiological or allegorical (as indeed Plutarch[4] suggests), to explain the importance of the goat in the mantic ritual of Delphi.[5] The real

[1] Vid. Diod. xvi. 26. Cf. Paus. x. v. 7 (with Frazer's " Comm.") ; Strabo, 419, 5.

[2] De Def. Orac. xlii. and xlvi.

[3] Some (e.g. Bouché-Leclercq, op. cit. iii. p. 74, n. 2) have taken the name Coretas to be etymologically connected with the Curetes and Crete, and hence have regarded it as a confirmation of the legend that the Delphic cult of Apollo was of Cretan origin.

[4] De Def. Orac. xlvi.

[5] The oracle was consulted after offering victims, especially

The Delphic Oracle

reason why Delphi was chosen as an oracular
shrine of Ge was, perhaps, not so much because of
its extraordinary natural impressiveness—though
indeed the wild grandeur of the scene would
naturally suggest the powers of Earth, and, for the
primitive Pelasgian,[1] make it peculiarly suitable
as a shrine of the chthonian divinities—as that it
had pre-eminently the elements requisite for a
shrine of Earth. What these elements are we shall
best see by considering briefly the Earth-oracle
of Dodona[2] and discussing its analogy with the

---

goats, vid. Diod. l.c. For omens from goats before consulting the oracle vid. Plut. De Def. Orac. xlvi. xlix. li.
Cf. Frazer's note to Paus. x. 5. 7. The importance of the
goat at Delphi is shown by numerous Delphic coins, on which
is the head of a goat, vid. " B. M. Catalogue of Gr. Coins (Central
Greece)," by B. V. Head (ed. by Poole), pp. 24–6. The same
is clear from the fact that the Delphic Omphalos was called
Ὀμφαλὸς Αἰγαῖος (vid. Hesych. s.v. Ὀμφαλὸς Αἰγός). Furthermore, the nurse of the Python at Delphi was known as Αἴξ
(vid. Plut. Quaest. Gr. 12).

[1] The Pelasgians (who must be regarded as strictly historical)
worshipped the great, unseen powers of Nature, to which at
first they assigned no particular names. Cf. Hdt. ii. 52.
For them " in their simplicity the voice of oak or rock sufficed,
if only they spoke the truth " (vid. Plat. Phaedr. 275,
τοῖς μὲν οὖν τότε ἅτε οὐκ οὖσι σοφοῖς, ὥσπερ ὑμεῖς οἱ νέοι, ἀπέχρη
δρυὸς καὶ πέτρας ἀκούειν, ὑπ᾽ εὐηθείας, εἰ μόνον ἀληθῆ λέγοιεν.) Yet
the Pelasgians seem to have been primitive only in religious
matters, for to them most probably must be assigned the
making of the great civilization known as Mycenaean or Minoan.
Vid. Ridgeway, " Early Age of Greece," vol. i. chap. 2.

[2] For the oracle of Dodona (which, according to Hdt. ii.
52, was accounted the most ancient of the oracles of Greece)
vid. Hdt. ii. 52 ff.; Serv. Aen. iii. 466; Cic. De Div. i. 76;

Pre-Apolline Cults of Delphi

oracle of Delphi. Here, I think, the Earth-goddess (who must be the Dione of Strabo) was, as at Delphi, the primary possessor of the Oracle, and the cult of Zeus was but a later accretion.[1] So great an authority as Dr. Farnell,[2] however, thinks it probable with Strabo[3] that the worship of Dione was attached to that of Zeus in a post-Homeric period. The argument he adduces is that there is no reference in Homer or Hesiod to her Dodonaean power or to her priestesses. The obvious answer is that an argument " from silence " is generally weak. This is particularly true in this case, at least in regard to Homer, who is all for the Olympian dynasty, and takes but scant account of the older stratum of religion to which Dione seems to have belonged. As

(and among modern writers) Bouché-Leclercq, op. cit. ii. pp. 278–301 ; Farnell, op. cit. i. pp. 38–40 ; Myers, " Essays," p. 22 ff. ; Jebb, App. to Soph. Tr. 1166 ; Smith, " Dict. of Ant." II. pp. 278-9, s.v. " Oraculum." The true site of Dodona was finally established by M. Constantin Carapanos in 1876. The results obtained by him are given in his work, " Dodone et ses Ruines," Paris, 1878.

[1] For the association of Zeus and the Earth-goddess at Dodona vid. verses ascribed to the priestesses (the Peleades) in Paus. x. 12. 10.

> Ζεὺς ἦν, Ζεὺς ἔστι, Ζεὺς ἔσσεται, ὦ μεγάλε Ζεῦ·
> Γᾶ καρποὺς ἀνίει· διὸ κλῄζετε Ματέρα Γαῖαν.

[2] "Cults," i. p. 39.

[3] 329. It seems quite possible that Strab. (never too critical) simply *borrows* his statement from Hom. Il. xvi. 233–5:

> Ζεῦ ἄνα, Δωδωναῖε, Πελασγικέ, τηλόθι ναίων κ.τ.λ.

The Delphic Oracle

regards Hesiod, silence in respect to Dione is
easily enough understood, for he refers to Dodona
only in two fragments, the one [1] containing only
one line, the other [2] twelve lines. If we had the
full context in these cases it is quite possible
that they would contain the name of Dione.
It must be conceded that the first explicit
mention of the worship of Dione at Dodona is
apparently in Demosthenes.[3] The *name* Dione
may be comparatively late, but that does not at
all prove that the worship of the Earth-goddess
was of late origin also. Doubtless the Pelasgian
Earth-goddess of Dodona—like Pelasgian deities
generally [4]—was nameless.

The following arguments might be adduced in
proof of the statement that the Earth-goddess
was the primary possessor of the oracle of Dodona.
In the first place, the modes of divination at Dodona
were such as one would expect to see associated
with the Earth-goddess—certainly not with the
sky-god, Zeus. These modes of divination consisted in the interpretation of the sounds in the

[1] Fr. 212 :

Δωδώνην φηγόν τε, Πελασγῶν ἕδρανον, ἦεν.

[2] Fr. 134 :

Ἔστι τις Ἑλλοπίη πολυλήιος ἠδ' εὐλείμων,
ἀφνειὴ μήλοισι καὶ εἰλιπόδεσσι βόεσσιν·
ἐν δ' ἄνδρες ναίουσι πολύρρηνες πολυβοῦται κ.τ.λ.

[3] Vid. Meid. p. 531, § 53.
[4] Vid. Hdt. II. 52.

12

Pre-Apolline Cults of Delphi

leaves [1]—the famous " speaking oaks " (αἱ προσήγοροι δρύες)—and of the babbling of the stream that trickled out from the roots of the oak-tree,[2] and the drawing of lots from the pitcher.[3] It is scarcely natural to associate such mantic methods with Olympian Zeus. Again, Zeus here alone was prominently an oracular god.[4] Other instances, such as the oracle of Zeus at Olympia, are obscure or doubtful.

Why was Zeus oracular here? The answer is : because of his association with Dione, and she is but the Earth-goddess, who was pre-eminently oracular.[5] Furthermore, the priestesses of Dodona, the Peleades,[6] seem to have been more prominent

[1] Aesch. P. V. 832 ; cf. Soph. Tr. 171, 1168 ; Hom. Od. xiv. 328, xix. 297 ; Plat. Phaedr. p. 275 B δρυὸς λόγοι; Luc. Amor. 31 ἡ ἐν Δωδώνῃ φηγὸς. . . . ἱερὰν ἀπορρήξασα φωνήν; Steph. Byz. s.v. Δωδώνη.

[2] Serv. Aen. iii. 466 (quoted by Farnell, " Cults," i. p. 143).

[3] Cic. De Div. i. 34, § 76.

[4] Vid. Farnell, op. cit. i. pp. 39–40.

[5] Vid. Bouché-Leclercq, op. cit. i. pp. 147, 182 ; ii. p. 15.

[6] For the Peleades (Πελειάδες, Πέλειαι), " doves," vid. Soph. Tr. 172, and Jebb's excellent note ; Paus. x. 12. 10 ; Hdt. ii. 55, 57 ; Strab. vii. Fr. i. (quoted by Jebb). Πέλειαι, according to Strabo, l.c., meant "aged women," being merely another form of Πολιαί. According to the view of Stein, the name was symbolical : these priestesses were called Πελειάδες (Πέλειαι), " Doves," as the Pythia and other priestesses were called Μέλισσαι, " Bees," with allusion to some sacred legend. Jebb thinks they were so called because the dove was sacred to Aphrodite, who was worshipped at Dodona as daughter of Zeus and Dione.

The Delphic Oracle

than the priests,[1] the Selloi[2] (" prophets of un-
washen feet, couching on the ground "). But this
is just what we should expect in the case of a shrine
of the Earth-goddess. Indeed, it seems quite
possible that here originally, as in Crete,[3] there was
a great goddess of fertility, of maternal character.
Afterwards, however, the Greeks associated with
her (as in the case of Rhea in Crete) the sky-god,

---

[1] Cf. Hdt. ii. 55, who makes no mention at all of the Selloi ;
surely he would have mentioned them if they were important ?
It is true that in Homeric times (vid. Hom. Il. xvi. 233 ff.)
there is no mention of the priestesses, but only of the *priests*,
the Selloi, who are "interpreters" (ὑποφῆται) of Zeus. This,
however, is only what we should expect. It is natural that
Hom. should ignore with the Earth-goddess her ministers as
well. Later times, however, saw a revival of the ancient
custom of having the Oracle served by priestesses.

[2] Il. xvi. 233 ff. Acc. to the Schol. on these lines, the
Selloi were a tribe dwelling at and around Dodona : he defines
them as ἔθνος Ἠπειρωτικόν ; vid. also Soph. Tr. 1166–7 ; Arist.
Meteor. I. 14, p. 352 b. 2.

[3] For the Nature-goddess of Crete vid. Evans, *M.T.P.C.*,
p. 70 ; R. M. Burrows, " Discoveries in Crete," p. 114 ; Bury,
" Hist. Gr." p. 19. It would seem that in the Mycenaean
(as well as in the later Phrygian) religion, the female aspect of
divinity was predominant. The male divinity, who usually
accompanies the goddess, is not so much her consort as her
son or youthful favourite. This is well shown by the scene
on a gold signet from the Acropolis Treasure at Mycenae. (For
a reproduction vid. Evans, *M.T.P.C.* p. 10, Fig. 4.) Here
evidently the seated goddess in the foreground is the principal
figure. The figure of the god (bearing the characteristic Mycenaean
shield) is relegated to the background. Evans suggests that
the divine pair may represent the sun and moon, figures of
which are represented at the top of the scene.

Pre-Apolline Cults of Delphi

Zeus, who took over her oracle and left her more or less a dim, shadowy figure.

That the Greeks at a very early date were intimate with Dodona and its Oracle is clear from the Homeric poems. Achaean Odysseus goes to Dodona " to hear the counsel of Zeus from the high leafy oak-tree of the god." [1] Telemachus extols his mother as " having no equal throughout the Achaean land, neither in sacred Pylos, nor in Argos, nor in Mycenae, nor yet in Ithaca, nor in the dark mainland " (*i.e.* Epirus).[2] Furthermore, the story of the Hyperboreans in Herodotus [3] makes it clear that in early times the only avenue between Greece and Upper Europe was that which started at Dodona and led up through Epirus to the head of the Adriatic, that is, towards Central Europe, whence according to the most probable view came the Achaean Greeks.[4] From all this we may safely conclude that at some very remote period the Greeks, having gained control of Dodona,[5]

---

[1] Vid. Od. xiv. 327–8 :

$$\tau\grave{o}\nu \ \delta' \ \grave{\epsilon}s \ \Delta\omega\delta\acute{\omega}\nu\eta\nu \ \phi\acute{a}\tau o \ \beta\acute{\eta}\mu\epsilon\nu\alpha\iota, \ \acute{o}\phi\rho\alpha \ \theta\epsilon o\hat{\iota}o$$
$$\grave{\epsilon}\kappa \ \delta\rho\upsilon\grave{o}s \ \acute{\upsilon}\psi\iota\kappa\acute{o}\mu o\iota o \ \Delta\iota\grave{o}s \ \beta o\upsilon\lambda\grave{\eta}\nu \ \grave{\epsilon}\pi\alpha\kappa o\acute{\upsilon}\sigma\alpha\iota. \ \kappa.\tau.\lambda.$$

[2] Vid. Od. xxi. 107–9.

[3] iv. 33.

[4] Vid. Ridgeway, " Early Age of Greece," I. chap. iv.

[5] Of this we have three proofs : (1) In the Hom. poems the Thesproti are in full occupation of South Epirus, which was called after them Thesprotia. But Thesprotia was merely a stage in the descent of the Achaeans from Upper Europe. Vid. Ridgeway, l.c. (2) The Σελλοί, or priests of Zeus at

The Delphic Oracle

associated their own Sky-god, Zeus, with the Pelasgic Earth-goddess, the primal possessor of the shrine. The fertilizing Rain-god, Zeus,[1] was a meet consort for Earth, sharing her temple (σύνναος) and appropriately worshipped under the title Νάϊος.[2]

With the association of Zeus and the Earth-goddess at Dodona we have a probable parallel in the case of the famous Labrandean Zeus of Caria,[3] whose symbol was the double-axe.[4] This he prob-

---

Dodona—who, as we have just seen, were a *tribe*—were also called Ἑλλοί by Pindar (vid. Schol. Il. l.c.). The district of Dodona is called by Hesiod (Fr. 134) Ἑλλοπίη or Ἐλλοπίη. Both Ἑλλοί and Ἑλλοπίη are obviously connected with Ἕλλην. (3) Aristotle (Meteor. I. 14, p. 352 b. 2), speaking of "the ancient Hellas" (τὴν Ἑλλάδα τὴν ἀρχαίαν), adds: αὕτη δ' ἐστὶν ἡ περὶ τὴν Δωδώνην καὶ τὸν Ἀχελῷον . . . ᾤκουν γὰρ οἱ Σελλοὶ ἐνταῦθα καὶ οἱ καλούμενοι τότε μὲν Γραικοὶ νῦν δ' Ἕλληνες.

[1] Cf. ὁ ὄμβριος Ζεύς, Strab. p. 718.

[2] For the epithet cf. the formula ἐπερωτῶντι τὸ κοινὸν τῶν . . . . Δία Νᾶον καὶ Διώναν which occurs on the leaden plates found by Carapanos in his excavations at Dodona (vid. "Dodone et ses Ruines," pp. 68–82, quoted by Jebb, App. to Soph. Tr. p. 206.

The word Νάϊος is best connected with √ of νάω, "flow," whence also come ἀέ-να-ος, νά-μα, Να-ϊάς, Νη-ϊάς, να-ρός, νη-ρός, Νη-ρεύς.

[3] For his temple vid. Hdt. v. 119.

[4] Vid. Evans, op. cit. p. 34 ; Ridgeway, "Early Age of Greece," I. p. 268 ; Frazer, "Comm. Paus." v. p. 308 (quoting B. V. Head, "Coins of the Ancients," iii. A. 33–5). The double-axe was associated also with Cretan Zeus. Numerous double-axes were found in the Dictaean Cave, when excavated by D. G. Hogarth. Many of them declare dedication to Cretan Zeus. Vid. Evans, op. cit. pp. 1, 13.

Pre-Apolline Cults of Delphi

ably borrowed from an older nature-cult similar
to that of Crete. A proof of the connexion between
the Carian and the old Cretan worship we have in
the name Labrandus, one of the Curetes who
migrated to Tralles.[1] The words Labrandus and
Labranda are surely connected with λάβρυς, or
" double-axe," the Cretan sacred symbol.[2] Labranda, like the Cretan Labyrinth, is the place of
the sacred λάβρυς, and Labrandeus is " he of the
double-axe."

It was natural of course that the Greeks, a
Northern, warlike, non-agricultural people, should
transfer the supremacy from a goddess to a god.
Certain elements of the old nature-worship, how-

[1] Vid. Evans, op. cit. p. 10.

[2] Vid. Evans, op. cit. p. 13, etc. Evans takes the " double-
axe " to be probably the symbol of the Cretan male-divinity
(who accompanies the goddess in the cult-scene already referred
to). Burrows, however, op. cit. p. 114, takes it to be a symbol
rather of the goddess. This latter view seems the more probable, for on a steatite gem from Cnossus the goddess is represented as holding the double-axe in her hand, and in the scene
from the signet-ring of Mycenae, just referred to, the double-
axe holds the central position just in front of the goddess.
I accept for the present Evans' interpretation of the Labyrinth as " the place of the double-axe " (λάβρυς). This derivation, however, is not by any means certain. For the Labyrinth
may well mean " the place of passages," the word being connected with λαύρα or λάβρα or λάϝρα, " passage " or " corridor."
(Cf. the Laura or " Arcade " in Samos and λαύρα or λάβρα, " a
monastery " in the early Eastern Church, being so called apparently because of its corridors.) Vid. Burrows, op. cit. p. 115 ;
R. S. Conway in App. to same. The interpretation of the
word Labyrinth, however, is quite immaterial to my argument.

The Delphic Oracle

ever, remained. Zeus of Dodona, as the verses of
the priestesses (already quoted) show, was regarded
as something physical and associated with the
perpetual fruitfulness of the earth. Probably, too,
the Peleades were a survival of the older cult of the
Nature-goddess.[1] They indeed may well mean
" Doves," deriving their name from the symbol
of the goddess, which here, as at Cretan Cnossus,[2]
was probably the dove. Finally, the oak may have
been a survival of the old-time tree-worship, which
was so prevalent in the Mycenaean age.[3]

The primary cult, then, at Dodona was, I think,
as at Delphi, the cult of the Earth-goddess. Let
us trace the analogy further. Corresponding with
the oak of Dodona there was at Delphi the laurel[4]
growing beside the cleft in the earth, which the
prophetess shook when delivering the oracles of
Apollo.[5] The laurel may well have been a relic of

[1] The Cretan Nature-goddess, too, seems to have been served
by priestesses, vid. Bury, " Hist. Gr." p. 19.

[2] Vid. Burrows, op. cit. p. 11. Cf. the snake-goddess of
Gournia, represented on a terra-cotta idol surrounded by a
snake, little doves and a three-legged altar (ibid. p. 27). For
the frequency of the dove in the art of the Mycenaean age vid.
Ridgeway, op. cit. pp. 8–11 ; Evans, op. cit. pp. 6–7.

[3] Vid. Evans, op. cit. passim.

[4] Vid. Ar. Plut. 213 : ὁ Φοῖβος αὐτὸς Πυθικὴν σείσας δάφνην·;
Schol. ibid. φασὶν ὡς πλησίον τοῦ τρίποδος δάφνη ἵστατο, ἣν ἡ
Πυθία, ἡνίκα ἐχρησμῴδει ἔσειεν. Cf. Paean of Ariston. (B.C.H.
xviii. p. 566), χλωρότομον δάφναν | σείων, where, however, the
epithet χλωρότομον shows that there is reference to a "fresh-
cut" branch.

[5] We are told in Eur. I.T. 1246, that a laurel stood beside

18

Pre-Apolline Cults of Delphi

tree-worship, having been once a prophetic tree like that of Dodona, its ancient prophetic character being represented afterwards by the Pythia's shaking it when she delivered her oracles. Again, as at Dodona, there was a spring, the spring Cassotis,[1] which was in connexion with an aqueduct plunging under the oracular cave, and from which the Pythia drank before mounting the prophetic tripod.[2] Corresponding with the drawing of lots from the pitcher at Dodona there was at Delphi the *thrioboly*, or divination by pebbles.[3] Unlike Dodona, however, there was at Delphi a cleft in the earth ($\chi\acute{a}\sigma\mu a$ $\gamma\hat{\eta}s$),[4] whence could ascend dreams, when there was a dream-oracle at Delphi,[5] and whence, too, at least in the opinion of later writers, ascended some mephitic vapour causing prophetic frenzy. We have, therefore, at Delphi all the elements necessary to constitute a shrine of Earth : a sacred tree, a fountain, a cleft in the ground, and withal a scenery of stern and awful majesty, where mountains and rocks seemed cleft as by some

the prophetic cave *before* Apollo took possession of Delphi. Cf. the legend given by Frazer, " Comm. Paus." x. 5. 5, which associates the laurel with Delphi before Apollo's coming.

[1] For Cassotis vid. Paus. x. 24. 7, where alone it is mentioned by name (vid. *B.C.H.* xvii. p. 619) ; Plut. De Pyth. Orac. xvii. (Cf. Foucart, " Mém. sur Delph." pp. 94–5.)

[2] Paus. ibid.

[3] For such divination at Delphi vid. infr. pp. 51–2.

[4] For a discussion of this famous cleft in the earth and the difficulties it raises vid. infr. pp. 59–60.

[5] For the dream-oracle at Delphi vid. Eur. I.T. 1260 ff.

The Delphic Oracle

giant hand, and where the repeated rumblings and shocks of earthquake seemed to bespeak the presence of the unseen powers of Nature.

Section B : Themis

What was the transition from Ge to Apollo? According to Aeschylus,[1] Themis succeeded her mother in the possession of the oracle, she in turn being succeeded by her sister Phoebe, the Titaness, who made a " birthday present " (γενέθλιον δόσιν) of her prophetic shrine and even of her name to Apollo. This story of Phoebe, however, sounds somewhat like a poetic contrivance of Aeschylus [2] —we find it nowhere else—to soften the transition from the telluric divinities to Apollo. Apart from the story of Phoebe, the history of the transition from Ge to Apollo, as given by Aeschylus, accords substantially with the statements of Pausanias,[3] Aristonous of Corinth in the Delphic Paean to Apollo,[4]

---

[1] Eum. 2. 4–8. Vid. supr. p. 1.

[2] Cf: Bouché-Leclercq, op. cit. iii. p. 46.

[3] x. 5. 6. Here we are told that Themis made a present directly to Apollo ('Απόλλωνα δὲ παρὰ Θέμιδος λαβεῖν δωρεάν) of the share of the shrine which she had inherited from Ge. The latter, though the original possessor of the oracle (x. 5. 5), had apparently afterwards shared it with Poseidon (x. 5. 6, the story being based on the Hymn of Musaeus).

[4] Vid. B.C.H. xvii. p. 566, Paean of Ariston. 20-1, πείσας (sc. 'Απόλλων) Γαῖαν, ἀνθοτρόφον | Θέμιν τ[ε] εὐπλόκαμον θεάν. A conflict, however, is faintly suggested in ἁγνισθείς, l. 16 (ibid.). If there had been no conflict, what need had Apollo of purification?

Pre-Apolline Cults of Delphi

Plutarch [1] and Strabo.[2] According to all these there was a peaceful succession of cults culminating in that of Apollo. There was, however, at Delphi another stratum of legend, which, while maintaining the same steps in the transition, maintained also that there was a mortal combat for the possession of Pytho—a combat of Earth through her symbol and protector the Python with the usurping Apollo.[3] Euripides [4] tells us how Apollo, having slain the dragon, " which protected the shrine of Earth," dismissed Earth's child, Themis, from the sanctuary and took possession of the oracle. Earth, however, to avenge her daughter, sent up dreams, " which revealed unto the cities of mortals the past and the future," thus thwarting and confusing the Apolline methods of consultation. The story doubtless illustrates a conflict of different cults and of different mantic processes at Delphi. This story of Apollo's taking possession of Delphi by force is alluded to by Apollodorus [5] and many other writers,[6] and it seems to have been the more prevalent form of the legend in the Greek world.

[1] De Def. Orac. xv. where he declares that the theologians of Delphi " wander very far from the truth who think that there the struggle once took place between the god and the snake for the possession of the oracle."

[2] 422.

[3] For a discussion of the " combat " and the relation of the Python to Earth vid. App. A.

[4] I.T. 1260 ff.

[5] Bibl. i. 4 (quoted by Farnell), op. cit. iv. p. 383.

[6] Cf. the references to the Python as " child of Earth " slain

The Delphic Oracle

According to legend, then, Themis was daughter of Earth. Now what concepts must we attach to her ? In general, she seems to have been the goddess of law and order, patroness of existing rites, in fine, justice personified.[1] In Homer, however, who mentions the goddess only thrice,[2] she has become like Hermes, " lackey of Zeus," summoning the gods to assembly,[3] convening and dismissing the assemblies of war,[4] presiding and keeping order at the banquets of the gods.[5] Hesiod names her in the *Theogony*[6] along with the Great Gods, and in the same poem[7] represents her as daughter of Uranus and Gaea. Pindar speaks of Themis as " having her seat beside the throne of Zeus,"[8] as " she who excelleth in counsel,"[9] as having for her daughter Eunomia,[10] and finally as " wise in counsel . . . primal spouse of the Saviour Zeus, with offspring the Hours that are ever true."[11]

by Apollo, Second Hymn to Ap. 28 [τ]ὸμ παῖδα Γâ[as] τ' ἔπεφνες ἰοῖς, *B.C.H.* xviii. p. 345 ff.; First Hymn to Ap. 20–2, *B.C.H.* xviii. pl. xxv (vid. App. A).

[1] Cf. Liddell and Scott, s.v. θέμιs.

[2] This is only what we should expect. For Themis (according to Hdt. ii. 50) was a purely Pelasgian divinity, and consequently in the eyes of the Homeric bard deserving but scant notice.

[3] Il. xx. 4.   [4] Od. ii. 68.
[5] Il. xv. 87 ff.   [6] 16.   [7] 135.
[8] O. viii. 21–2.

> ἔνθα σώτειρα Διὸς ξενίου
> πάρεδρος ἀσκεῖται Θέμιs.

[9] O. xiii. 11.   [10] O. ix. 16.
[11] Fr. 29–30 (Bergk); vid. Sandys' " Pindar " (Loeb), p. 514.

Pre-Apolline Cults of Delphi

Aeschylus regards her as one of the older divinities before the reign of Zeus, identifying her with Gaea, both being " but one form with many names" (πολλῶν ὀνομάτων μορφὴ μία).[1] She is "right-counselling " (ὀρθόβουλος), with Prometheus as her son.[2]

Following Aeschylus we may regard Themis as identical with Ge, of whom she seems but an idealized form, due to the working of the Greek religious imagination.[3] Why, then, did Ge acquire the appellative Themis ? The title originally seems to have designated, not so much the goddess of right-eousness—that is probably a comparatively later notion—as the goddess of prophecy : she is prophecy personified, for θέμις as a common noun was frequently used to designate the decrees of the gods as declared by oracles.[4] Yet the idea of righteous-

The fragment is remarkable as belonging to one of the poet's earliest compositions. It was so full of mythological allusions that the poetess Corinna, who had suggested his turning attention to mythology, told him " to sow with the hand, not with the whole sack " (Sandys' note).

[1] P.V. 210. Because of this identification of Themis with Ge, she was sometimes represented with the *cornu copiae*, as goddess of plenty and fertility.

[2] Ibid. 18, cf. also 874.

[3] Cf. Farnell, op.cit. iii. p. 131; Miss Harrison, "Themis," p. 387.

[4] θέμις, from √ΘΕ, seen in τίθημι, is the same as our word " doom " (A.S. dôm), i.e. " judgment." Cf. Skt. *dhâ-man* (*seat, law, custom*), O.H.G. *tuom*, Goth. *doms*. Its meaning, then, as decree of the gods, oracle, was quite a natural one. For this use cf. Hom. Hymn. Ap. 394 (θεμίστας Φοίβου Ἀπόλλωνος); Od. xvi. 403 ; Pind. P. iv. 96.

ness is not at all excluded. If θέμις is the decree of Heaven manifested in oracles, then Θέμις must embody the idea of righteousness, for the decrees of Heaven must be righteous. In applying the cult-epithet Θέμις,[1] then, to Ge, the Greeks meant to designate the oracular goddess as the mouth-piece (προφῆτις) of the righteous ordinances of Zeus—as it was meet that she should be, being, as Pindar says, " his primal spouse " (ἀρχαίαν ἄκοιτιν).

SECTION C : POSEIDON

But what has the sea-god, Poseidon, " he of the gleaming trident " ('Αγλαοτριαίνης), to do with the oracular shrine of Delphi ? Certain it is at least that he had some footing at Parnassus and " the sacred city." But whether his cult struck deep at Delphi or not in ancient times we cannot maintain with certainty. One writer [2] has maintained the identity of the Delphic month Ποϊτρόπιος with the Ionic Ποσειδεών,[3] asserting that, though in later times it was sacred to Dionysus, yet anciently it must

---

[1] There was a cult of Γῆ Θέμις at Athens, vid. *C.I.A.* iii. 3, 350 (on seat in theatre), ἱερίας Γῆς Θέμιδος ; vid. Farnell, op. cit. iii. p. 309.

[2] A. Mommsen, " Delphika," p. 278 : " In historischen Zeit gehörte der Poitropios zu den bakchischen Monaten, vor Alters ist er vermutlich ein Monat des Poseidon gewesen, etc." His view is followed by Hiller von Gaertringen, *P.W.* s.v." Delphoi," 2527.

[3] Ποσειδεών was the sixth month of the Athenian year (corresponding with the second part of our Dec. and the first part of Jan.) and used by Ionians generally.

Pre-Apolline Cults of Delphi

have belonged to Poseidon. If this were true, we should have a striking proof of the early importance of the Poseidon cult at Delphi. The month Ποϊτρόπιος is perhaps the month of "solemn supplication,"[1] and we know that offerings were made to Poseidon in this month,[2] but we cannot maintain with any certainty that the month Ποϊτρόπιος was named from these offerings.

A more reliable proof we have in the statement of Pausanias,[3] who bases his account upon the poem of Musaeus, that Poseidon possessed the Oracle in common with Ge before Apollo's arrival at Delphi ; that Earth gave responses in person, while Poseidon employed a certain Pyrkon[4] as his representative. Pausanias goes on to say that Earth

---

[1] I should suggest that the first part of the word, ποι = ποτι, the intersonantic T being dropped by a Doric peculiarity as in κέραος, τέραος, etc., for κέρατος, τέρατος, etc. (For a similar dialectic suppression in modern Greek, e.g. τοῦο for τοῦτο, vid. Jannaris, " Hist. Gr. Gr." p. 87.) Ποϊτρόπιος, then, would be = ποτιτρόπιος, Dor. for προστρόπαιος, " turning to (a god or man) in solemn supplication " (esp. for purification). Ποτιτρόπαιος is used in Aesch. Eum. 176, in the sense of " one defiled " (ἐναγής).

[2] *C.I.G.* 523, 18..   [3] x. 5. 6.

[4] Pyrkon, or Pyrkaon, is very probably the symbol of empyromancy, from πῦρ and κάων. There were at Delphi priests called Πυρκόοι, who divined by means of omens from burnt offerings ; vid. Frazer, " Comm. Paus." x. 5. 6 (quoting from Hesychius). They may have been priests of Poseidon, who had an altar at Delphi. They may, however, have been priests of Prometheus, the Fire-god. For Prometheus' connexion with Delphi vid. Mommsen, op. cit. p. 256 ff. It is noteworthy that the Pythia calls the Delphians Πυρικάοι, vid. Plut. De Pyth. Orac. xxiv.

25

The Delphic Oracle

resigned her share of the Oracle to Themis, who
made a present of it to Apollo, while Poseidon got
from Apollo the island of Calauria [1] off Troezen, in
exchange for his share of the Oracle.[2] The recently-
discovered Delphic Paean of Aristonous speaks of
Poseidon as presenting Apollo with his own " holy
ground," on the latter's arrival at Delphi.[3] There
are, furthermore, two legends connecting Poseidon
with Delphi. According to the one,[4] Mt. Parnassus
was named after Parnassus, a son of Poseidon and
the nymph Cleodora. According to the other,
Delphi was named from Delphus, son of Poseidon
and the nymph Melaena or Melantho.[5]

Certainly in later times at least Poseidon held a
prominent place in Delphic religion. We learn from
Aeschylus [6] that the Pythia invoked him before
she took her seat upon the tripod. Pausanias [7]

[1] Acc. to Strab. 374, Pos. got Taenarum.

[2] Epithet of Pos. ('Αμοιβεύς) at Delphi (vid. Farnell, op. cit.
iv. p. 27) possibly refers to this legend. Farnell (ibid.), however, thinks this unlikely.

[3] Vid. ll. 33–4 (B.C.H. xvii. p. 566; O. Crusius, "Die Delphischen Hymnen," Phil. '94, p. 5) : Δωροῦνται δέ σ[ε] ἀθάνατοι
Ποσειδῶν ἀγνοῖς δαπέδοις, κ.τ.λ.

[4] Paus. x. 6. 1.

[5] Vid. Frazer, " Comm. Paus." x. 6. 4 (quoting Tzetzes,
Schol. Lycophr. 208). Melaena here is probably "the black
Earth " (μέλαινα, sc. Γῆ).

[6] Eum. 27:

Πλείστου τε πηγὰς καὶ Ποσειδῶνος κράτος | καλοῦσα κ.τ.λ.

[7] x. 24. 4. Farnell, op. cit. iv. p. 27, thinks that the epithet
Προνέως, applied by Hesychius to Pos. at Delphi, may refer
to this. This, however, does not seem natural, for Pausanias

Pre-Apolline Cults of Delphi

tells us that Poseidon had an altar in the temple. A recently-discovered inscription at Delphi speaks of the " precinct of Poseidon " (τὸ Ποτειδάνιον) on the terrace above the Pythium.[1]

Whence came to Delphi the worship of Poseidon ? It does not seem to have come by sea, for there is no legend pointing in that direction ; nor is there any trace of his cult on the shore of Cirrha. Most probably, then, it came by land, either from Boeotia [2] or from Thessaly,[3] in either case probably through Minyan influence.

distinctly says that the altar stood " *in* the temple " (ἐν τῷ ἱερῷ), not " in front " of it. Dr. Verrall suggested that what Paus. meant really was the Omphalos (Eur. Ion, Introd. p. xlvi). Well, perhaps Paus. was mistaken, but we have now no means of disproving his statement or of proving Verrall's.

[1] Vid. *B.C.H.* xvi. p. 65.

[2] This was a great centre of the Poseidon cult ; cf. the cult of Pos. Ἑλικώνιος, which held together the Ionian Confederacy (vid. Strab. 384). This epithet was derived from Mt. Helicon in Boeotia, not, as used to be thought, from the Achaean town Ἑλίκη (vid. Farnell, op. cit. iv. p. 29 ff.).

[3] Farnell, op. cit. p. 28, thinks it more probable that the cult of Poseidon at Delphi was of Thessalian origin. He bases his statement on the famous inscr. of the Labyadae (vid. *B.C.H.* xix. p. 25). The Labyadae were Thessalian, because (1) Poseidon is called Φράτριος, a title of the god found nowhere else. (2) The Labyadae officials were known as Ταγοί, a term peculiarly Thessalian. (3) Certain words, e.g. δάρατα, " sacrificial cakes," occur in the text, which are also peculiar to Thessaly.

Yet these arguments do not seem conclusive. Granted that the Labyadae were Thessalian, and granted that the epithet Φράτριος is almost exclusively confined to Thessaly in reference to Poseidon, it does not necessarily follow that the cult of Poseidon at Delphi came from Thessaly. Finding Poseidon

The Delphic Oracle

How came Poseidon to be connected with the Oracle of Delphi ? It is noteworthy that nowhere else is Poseidon an oracular god, but of course there is no intrinsic reason why any deity of the Pantheon might not become on occasion the source of divination, especially at Delphi. Perhaps the fact that Delphi was situated near the sea and was subject at all times to earthquakes [1] made it natural that " the Earth-Shaker" ('$E\nu o\sigma i\chi\theta\omega\nu$, '$E\nu\nu o\sigma i\gamma a\iota o\varsigma$) should be there worshipped.

The true explanation, however, is possibly to be sought in another direction. In origin the Poseidon cult was most probably Pelasgian.[2] Proof of this we have in the fact that the great centres of the

at Delphi the Labyadae would naturally address him with the title with which they addressed him at home. It may well be that the Poseidon cult was introduced at Delphi from its great neighbouring stronghold—Boeotia.

[1] Cf. Mommsen, op. cit. p. 14. Philostr. (Apollon. of Tyana, vi. 41) says that a sacrifice was proposed to be made to Poseidon and Ge conjointly, " when the cities on the left-hand side of the Hellespont were afflicted by earthquakes." Cf. Diod. xvi. 56. Delphi is subject to earthquakes also in modern times. There was a very severe one there in 1870 ; cf. B.C.H. xviii. p. 178, where it is stated that the excavations were interrupted by earthquakes in '93.

[2] The Pelasgians must be regarded as strictly historical, vid. Ridgeway (op. cit. I. p. 88), who agrees with the views of Niebuhr, Thirlwall, Grote, E. Curtius, L. R. Farnell, etc. To them, as has been already pointed out, most probably must be attributed the making of that great civilization, known as Mycenaean or Minoan, from which the veil was partially removed by the excavations of Schliemann, and yet further by the work of Evans in Crete. Vid. Ridgeway, op. cit. I. chap. ii.

Pre-Apolline Cults of Delphi

Poseidon worship coincide ethnically with the Pelasgian areas. The Minyans of Thessaly were the chief Poseidon worshippers,[1] but the Minyans were of the Pelasgic stock.[2] Boeotia, too, as we have just seen, was a great centre of the worship of Poseidon, and thence came Poseidon Ἑλικώνιος,[3] the chief divinity of the Ionian Confederacy. This of course is only what we should expect, for the Ionians were themselves Pelasgic in origin.[4] Arcadia, according to Hesiod[5] and Pausanias,[6] was a great Pelasgic centre, and Poseidon was the predominant Arcadian god.[7]

Poseidon, then, being very probably in origin a Pelasgic divinity, it seems quite reasonable to maintain with Pausanias[8] that at an early date he was associated with Ge at Delphi. The association was a natural one, the fertilizing water-god[9]

[1] Vid. Farnell, op. cit. iv. p. 26 ff. There was a decided Minyan strain in the Boeotian cult. Onchestus and Haliartus were the chief Minyan cities, with which the worship of Poseidon was connected.

[2] Vid. Ridgeway, op. cit. I. pp. 116, 167.

[3] Vid. p. 27, n. 2. For the Ionians in Boeotia vid. Hdt. v. 58.

[4] Vid. Hdt. i. 56; cf. Ridgeway, op. cit. I. p. 124.

[5] Apud Strab. v. p. 221, τῷ δ' Ἐφόρῳ τοῦ ἐξ Ἀρκαδίας εἶναι τὸ φῦλον τοῦτο (τοὺς Πελασγούς) ἦρξεν Ἡσίοδος· φησὶ γὰρ " υἱεῖς— Πελασγός."

[6] viii. 1. 4. The Pelasgians of Thessaly came from Arcadia (vid. Ridgeway, op. cit. I. p. 232).

[7] Vid. Ridgeway, op. cit. I. p. 124.

[8] x. 5. 6. Cf. x. 24. 4, ἐν δὲ τῷ ναῷ πεποίηται μὲν Ποσειδῶνος βωμός, ὅτι τὸ μαντεῖον τὸ ἀρχαιότατον κτῆμα ἦν καὶ Ποσειδῶνος.

[9] The best etymology connects the name Ποσειδῶν with

The Delphic Oracle

being regarded as a meet consort of the Earth-goddess. So, too, Poseidon was associated with the Tilphossian Erinys in the territory of Minyan Haliartus and with Thelpousan Demeter in Arcadia, both being merely disguised forms of Ge.[1]

SECTION D : DIONYSUS

Was the cult of Dionysus at Delphi pre-Apolline ? When did that divinity first gain a footing on Parnassus ? Bouché-Leclercq,[2] whose view is followed by Miss Harrison,[3] maintains that Dionysus preceded Apollo at Delphi. These are his words : " Le culte de Dionysos était si fortement implanté sur le Parnasse, si bien attaché au sol par son association avec les Nymphes, qu'il n'en put être arraché par la religion apollinienne." But this view is very doubtful. In the first place, let us

√ΠΟ which appears in πόσις, ποτόν, ποταμός. Indeed it would seem that Poseidon was originally god of *fresh* water, rather than of the sea. Cf. Lat. *Neptunus*, connected with the name of the Etruscan town *Nepete*, which is itself connected with the Umbrian word *nepitu*, meaning " flood." (Vid. R. S. Conway in *C.R.* vol. xxxi. no. 1, p. 17.) A. Mommsen, " Delphika," p. 7, would connect the first part of the word Ποσειδῶν with √ΠΑ, which appears in Skt. *pat-is*, " lord," " husband," Lat. *potis*, *possum*, etc., Gr. πόσις (orig. πότις), " husband," πότνια, " mistress," " queen." Ποσειδῶν according to this etymology would simply = " lord."

For Poseidon as vegetation-deity, with the title Φυτάλμιος, " nurturer," vid. Paus. ii. 32. 8 ; *C.I.G.* iii. 269.

[1] Vid. Farnell, op. cit. iv. p. 27.
[2] Op. cit. i. p. 353, cf. ibid. iii. 51.
[3] " Proleg." p. 560.

examine the argument which the writer advances. "The domineering character of the Apolline priesthood, whose constant aim was to destroy or else divert to the profit of its own divinity all anterior tradition, would not," he says, "have allowed the cult of Dionysus to invade a place already chosen and occupied by Apollo." This reasoning is hardly sound. Is it not more reasonable to maintain that the Apolline priesthood, possessed as it was of an uncommon degree of sagacity, received with open arms a cult which had already triumphed in other parts of Greece, and which bade fair to progress still further, whether Delphi willed or not ? That this is the only reasonable view is based on two considerations. In the first place, the statement that Dionysus preceded Apollo at Delphi rests on very slight evidence indeed. It rests practically on the statement of a late scholiast.[1] The Delphic Paean of Aristonous, it is true, speaks of Dionysus as presenting Apollo, on the latter's coming to Delphi, with his own " triennial torch-processions."[2] The Paean, however, is comparatively late,[3] having been written

---

[1] Schol. Arg. Pind. P.: Πυθῶνος δὲ τότε κυριεύσαντος τοῦ προφητικοῦ τρίποδος, ἐν ᾧ πρῶτος Διόνυσος ἐθεμίστευσε. This sounds like a late Orphic exaggeration. The statement in Macrob., i. 18, 3 (vid. Farnell, op. cit. v. p. 290), which is sometimes adduced in proof of the precedence of Dionysus at Delphi, merely proves the subsequent union of the two cults.

[2] Vid. l. 37 (B.C.H. xvii. p. 566 ; O. Crusius, op. cit. p. 5), . . . τριετέσιν φαναῖς Βρόμιος.

[3] It probably belongs to one of the first three centuries B.C.

The Delphic Oracle

at a time when " Bromius held the place " at Delphi, and was so firmly established there that he might well seem even the forerunner of Apollo. The Homeric poems,[1] however, and the Homeric Hymn to Apollo show no trace of the worship of Dionysus at Delphi.

The argument from silence, it is true, in this case has not much force : are these poems not equally silent about the cult of Ge ? But it has decided weight in the case of Aeschylus[2] and Pausanias,[3] who set themselves to give the history of the Oracle from pre-Apolline times to their own day. Yet those writers never mention Dionysus as having at any period, anterior or subsequent to Apollo's arrival at Delphi, possessed the Oracle. Equally silent are Strabo and Diodorus. Finally the diffusion of the Apolline worship is a far earlier phenomenon in Greek religious history than the invasion of the Dionysiac cult.[4] Why, then, should we invert the order at Delphi, where we know that the Apolline worship was firmly installed

Cf. Weil, *B.C.H.* xvii. p. 561. Crusius, op. cit. pp. 26–8, would put the date of its composition somewhat earlier— *circ.* 400 B.C.

[1] Dionysus in the Iliad cuts more or less a sorry figure. Cf. Il. vi. 135–6, where he is represented as flying in terror from Lycurgus.

[2] Eum. 1 ff. It is true that Aesch. (ibid. 24) says that " Bromius holds the place " (Βρόμιος δ' ἔχει τὸν χῶρον). Yet this does not mean that Dionysus had possession of the *Oracle*, but that his cult flourished vigorously there.

[3] x. 5.   [4] Vid. Farnell, op. cit. v. p. 113.

Pre-Apolline Cults of Delphi

in the days of Homer,[1] when Dionysus was as yet a poltroon?

In origin the Dionysus cult seems to have been Thraco-Phrygian, having been carried by Phrygian migration from Thrace into Asia-Minor. From the Balkan districts it spread into Macedonia and certain northern Greek communities, notably the Minyans of Thessaly and Boeotia. By the Minyans of Boeotia it was probably brought to Delphi.[2]

But the cult of Dionysus, no matter when or whence introduced, rapidly grew in importance at Delphi till eventually he became almost the compeer of Apollo.[3] To his service were devoted the three months of winter during Apollo's ἀποδημία.[4]

---

[1] Cf. Il. ix. 404–5; Od. viii. 79.

[2] I follow in this question the conclusions of Farnell, op. cit. v. p. 89 ff.

[3] Cf. Plut. De E apud Delph. ix. . . . πρὸς τὸν Διόνυσον, ᾧ τῶν Δελφῶν οὐδὲν ἧττον ἢ τῷ Ἀπόλλωνι μέτεστιν. Cf. also B.C.H. xix. p. 93, Delphic Paean to Dionysus, 71, where Dionysus is declared the brother of Apollo, θ[ε]ῶν ἱερῶι γένει συναίμωι. The same friendly relations are shown in B.C.H. xviii. p. 355, Second Hymn to Ap. 39, where Ap. is asked to protect the "servants of Dionysus." Cf. the Gr. vase found at Kertsch, 1860, showing Apollo and Dionysus shaking hands before a palm-tree. Acc. to Philochorus, Fr. 22 (quoted by Evans, M.T.P.C., p. 22), the tomb of Dionysus stood at Delphi beside the golden image of Apollo. Acc. to Tatian, Adv. Graec. viii. 25, the Omphalos was the tomb of Dionysus, ὁ δὲ ὀμφαλὸς τάφος ἐστι Διονύσου. For the relations of Dionysus with Apollo at Delphi vid. Farnell, op. cit. v. pp. 112–14; P.W. s.v. Apollon, 35.

[4] Then the dithyramb was substituted for the paean (Plut. De E apud Delph. ix.).

The Delphic Oracle

Indeed the union of the two divinities at last became so complete that at times the personality of the one seems to merge in that of the other. They exchange epithets,[1] and Apollo becomes the eager propagandist of the cult of his brother god.[2] The Thyiads, " the wild women " of Delphi, rave in the service of Dionysus and Apollo in mid-winter on the heights of Parnassus.[3] The Bacchic frenzy assumes the prophetic nature.[4] At no period, however, does Apollo seem to have shared with Dionysus the oracular function. This privilege, too, he refused to his brother, Hermes " of the golden wand," for it was a prerogative incommunicably his own.[5]

[1] Vid. ὁ Κισσεὺς 'Απόλλων ὁ Βάκχειος ὁ μάντις, quoted from Aesch., and δέσποτα φιλόδαφνε Βάκχε, Παιὰν ΅Απολλον εὔλυρε, quoted from Eur. (Fr. 480) by Macrob. i. 18. 3. Cf. Delphic Paean to Dionysus (*B.C.H.* xix. p. 393), where at the end of each stanza Dionysus is addressed as Παιάν, e.g. 'Ιὲ Παιάν, ἴθι σωτή[ρ]. In l. 71 Dionysus is declared brother of Apollo.

[2] For this propagation of the Dionysus cult vid. infr. pp. 117–19. For the relations of the " Hosii " with Dionysus vid. App. B.

[3] Vid. Paus. x. 32. 7, 6. 4 ; Plut. 953 D. Cf. Lucan, Phars. v. 73, "mons Phoebo Bromioque sacer." Attic women joined in' these orgiastic rites, vid. Paus. x. 4. 3. For references in the poets vid. Soph. Ant. 1127–9 :

> σὲ δ' ὑπὲρ διλόφου πέτρας στέροψ ὄπωπε
> λιγνύς, ἔνθα Κωρύκιαι
> στείχουσι Νύμφαι Βακχίδες, κ.τ.λ.

Cf. Eur. Ion, 1125–6 ; Ar. Nub. 603.

[4] Cf. Eur. Bacch. 298–9, Τὸ γὰρ βακχεύσιμον | καὶ τὸ μανιῶδες μαντικὴν πολλὴν ἔχει ; Eur. Tiresias (Fr.), 298, μάντις δ' ὁ δαίμων ὅδε.

[5] Vid. Hom. Hymn. Merc. 534 ff.

Pre-Apolline Cults of Delphi

Section E : Apollo's Coming to Delphi

Such were the predecessors of Apollo in the great shrine on " rocky Pytho "; such the cults Apollo found there installed when he came from his Northern home. When exactly Apollo came to Delphi it is impossible to say : all that can with safety be asserted is that Apollo's coming took place at some very early epoch in the Hellenic period before the movement of the tribes across the sea, probably even before the Peloponnesus was fully Hellenized. The antiquity of the Apolline oracle is proved, in the first place, by the constitution of the Amphictyonic Council,[1] which goes back to a very early period ; secondly, by its wealth, which was proverbial even in the days of Homer ; [2] and finally by the fact that it seems to have flourished in the Mycenaean age, undoubted traces of a Minoan settlement having been found at Delphi.[3]

[1] For the Amphictyonic Council vid. Strab. 420, Paus. x. 8. 1 ; Aeschin. De Fals. Leg. 115 ; Freeman, " History of Federal Gov." chap. iii. ; Grote, " Hist. Gr." vol. iii. p. 34 ff., vol. xi. pp. 217-8.

[2] Il. ix. 404-5.

[3] The lion's head in porcelain found at Delphi is in perfect agreement in style and technique with the lions' heads found by Evans at Cnossus (vid. Farnell, op. cit. iv. p. 185, note). A double-axe—the Minoan religious symbol—has also been found by the French excavators, vid. M. H. Swindler, op. cit. p. 16 (quoting *B.P.W.* 1896, 1086). For Mycenaean vases, swords, etc., found also by the French, vid. *B.C.H.* xviii. p. 195. For the rock-hewn, bee-hive tomb found by the French excavators

The Delphic Oracle

Attracted, perhaps, by the growing fame of the Oracle—for oracle it seems to have been long before Apollo's coming—the Apolline tribe seized and transformed it. It is probable that the Oracle was first the possession of a single tribe, and that the Dorian. For, although Apollo seems to have been originally a Hellenic god, common to all the Hellenic tribes, he was the peculiar god—the tribal god in fact—of the Dorians.[1] It is not unlikely that Pytho was seized by the Dorians,[2] who thence spread the Apolline worship through the Peloponnesus. As proof of the latter statement we have the fact that Arcadia, which remained outside the sphere of Dorian influence, is practically lacking in independent Apolline cults. This is the view long ago propounded by K. O. Müller.[3] Müller,

at Delphi like that of Gortyna in Crete vid. Ridgeway, op. cit. I. p. 40. Furthermore, the idea of two eagles on either side of the Omphalos at Delphi is most probably due to Mycenaean or Minoan influence: the device of two animals, etc., ranged heraldically on either side of a tree or pillar, is a distinctively Mycenaean motive. An excellent example of this heraldic grouping of figures we have in the famous " Lion Gate " of Mycenae. Here we see two lions facing each other, between which is a vertical pillar (tapering towards its base). Vid. Ridgeway, op. cit. I. pp. 4, 279–81 ; Evans, *M.T.P.C.* pp. 3, 19, etc. According to Evans, op. cit. pp. 54, 64, this scheme is essentially Egyptian in origin.

[1] Cf. Grote, " Hist. Gr." i. p. 44.

[2] Cf. Bury, " Hist. Gr." p. 61. This would best account for the close connexion which always existed between Delphi and Sparta, for instances of which vid. infr. p. 84, n. 6.

[3] Vid. "Dorians" (Trans.), i. p. 228.

Pre-Apolline Cults of Delphi

however, seems incorrect in saying that migrations
of the Greek tribes before the Dorians took no part
in the spread of the Apolline cult, for it is highly
probable that there were pre-Dorian cults of Apollo
in the Peloponnesus.[1]

[1] For the cults of Ἀπόλλων Πυθαεύς, Κάρνειος, Λύκειος, which were
established there by older Dryopian settlements, vid. Farnell,
op. cit. iv. pp. 111–12.

CHAPTER II

THE INFLUENCE OF THE APOLLINE ORACLE OF DELPHI: ITS CAUSES

SECTION A: EXTENT OF THE DELPHIC INFLUENCE

How silent now is the Oracle of " rocky Pytho " ! Its temple is ruined, its priestess forgotten ; not a trace is left of its ancient splendour save only the remnants that have been brought to light by the hand of the excavator.[1]   Yet in olden times it was a great religious centre to which pilgrims flocked from all parts of the world.   Greek and barbarian alike consulted it : envoys came from Asia and Libya and distant Italy seeking advice on all matters of moment.   The framing of laws, the founding of colonies, the making and unmaking of kings, the beginning of wars, the healing of disease or pesti-

[1] The systematic exploration of the site of Delphi (begun by Müller and Curtius in 1840, continued in 1860 by Wescher and Foucart, resumed by Haussoullier in 1880) was completed by the French School, 1892–98. So thoroughly did the last excavators, headed by Homolle (who had the assistance of Colin, Couve, Bourguet, Perdrizet, Fournier and Laurent), set to work, that they actually removed the village of Kastri, which stood on the site of the ancient Delphi, and rebuilt it on another spot.

The Influence of the Apolline Oracle

lence [1]—these and such-like questions were submitted to the unerring judgment of the omniscient
Apollo. From the earliest times the Oracle of
Delphi influenced the history of noble houses, aye,
and of whole nations. The Delphic Oracle of
Apollo, as no other oracle of antiquity, long inspired a living faith, and for centuries retained its
credit unimpaired. Its responses were received
with implicit faith, even when they led a Croesus
or a Pyrrhus to his doom.[2]

Great, however, as was the influence of the
Delphic Oracle, nevertheless in matters political it
had considerable limitations. The word of Apollo,
so potent for making or unmaking kings, dynasties
and laws, rested almost exclusively on moral
authority.[3] It did not, could not, prescribe any
coercive means for having its mandates obeyed. It

[1] For instances of all such consultation vid. infr. chaps.
iii, iv, v. Cf. Plut. De Def. Orac. xlvi, De Pyth. Orac.
xxvi; Cic. De Div. i. 3, "quod bellum susceptum ab ea (i.e.
Graecia) sine consilio deorum est ? "

[2] For ambiguous oracles, misinterpretation of which led
Croesus and Pyrrhus to undertake ruinous projects, vid. infr.
p. 66 and n. 4.

[3] Occasionally, of course, its cause would be championed by
the " secular arm," now by the Amphictyonic Council, now by
the Spartans or Macedonians. For the Amphictyonic Council's
championing the Delphic Oracle in the First Sacred War vid.
Grote, "Hist. Gr." vol. iii. pp. 37–8. The Spartans were the
unfailing friends and supporters of the Pythian shrine (vid. infr.
p. 84). Philip of Macedon, in the Second Sacred War, proclaimed himself the champion of the Delphic god, and the avenger
of the despoiling of his shrine, vid. Justin, viii. 2, " Igitur
Philippus, quasi sacrilegii, non Thebanorum ultor esset, omnes

39

gave counsels which cities and individuals followed or neglected at their own risk and peril. The Delphic authority was efficacious only on condition of its not exacting obedience. The Delphic Oracle made little or no effort to promote political unity. Indeed, its priesthood probably recognized that any such efforts would have been doomed to failure. Such was the Greek temperament that for the Greek races political unity was impossible, the reason being, as Bury well remarks, that " the Panhellenic idea was weaker than the love of local independence." [1] The Oracle, as a rule, had little influence in the matter of initiation. Greek states generally did not ask Apollo to originate their policy : they merely sought his sanction for what they had already determined upon, and invoked his blessing upon a project already conceived. But, if the Delphic Oracle failed to produce political unity, it succeeded amply in promoting unity of another kind—ideal unity, the unity of religion.[2]

Yet apart from such limitations as we have just mentioned, the Oracle of Delphi, at least at its zenith, wielded a very great influence, an influence all the more surprising when we bear in mind how

milites coronas laureas sumere iubet, atque ita, veluti deo duce, in proelium pergit. . . . Illum vindicem sacrilegii, illum ultorem religionum etc." We shall see, however (infr. pp. 166–7), that the Macedonian patronage proved more a curse than a blessing for the Oracle.

[1] " Hist. Gr." p. 161.

[2] For the influence of the Oracle in bringing about religious unity vid. infr. chap. iv.

The Influence of the Apolline Oracle

deeply the Greek loved in all things local autonomy. Certainly there must have been strong reasons which made Delphi a Panhellenic centre of divinations,[1] breaking down racial barriers, substituting one central, irresponsible authority for the system of free divination—the divination of a Calchas or a Tiresias, which was more in conformity with national habits and glorified by the memories of the heroic age.

Section B: Causes of the Influence of the Oracle

It remains for us, then, to consider the causes of this influence. Now these causes may be reduced to two main divisions, the one extrinsic, the other intrinsic to the Apolline religion itself. Among the extrinsic causes first should be placed what may be termed the historico-religious cause —the old religious associations of the shrine. The sanctity of Pytho was of no recent date : its religious history stretched away into the dim, distant past. Cult after cult there flourished,[2] till at last came that of Apollo, the crown and completion of them all.[3] Little wonder, then, is it that

---

[1] Cf. τρίποδα κοινὸν Ἑλλάδος (Eur. Ion, 366) ; κοινὴ ἑστία (Plut. Arist. 20, Ael. Var. Hist. iv. 6, vid. infr. p. 165) ; " commune humani generis oraculum " (Liv. xxxviii. 48) ; cf. Bury, " Hist. Gr." p. 160.

[2] What these cults were we have already seen in chap, i.

[3] For this superimposing of the Apolline cult on the preceding cults at the Delphic shrine we have many parallels in history. St. Christophorus was substituted for Trophonius at the shrine

The Delphic Oracle

in the eyes of the Greeks Pytho was "hallowed," ἠγαθέη,[1] in the highest sense. And the influence of the Oracle was due in no small measure to the excellence of the Apolline religion, which gathered up in itself the heritage of all the traditions associated with the place, and retained certain elements from all the cults.

The prestige of the Oracle was heightened probably also by the Delphic association with the Hyperboreans.[2] These were no mysterious folk, a blessed people, living long lives of innocence and ease in a far-away land of perpetual sunshine, as the poets [3] loved to depict them, but real, Northern Greek ministers of Apollo, who performed certain sacred functions for Northern Hellas. The old derivation as the "dwellers beyond the North wind"—for which Pindar [4] and Herodotus [5] are our earliest authorities—is now discarded, and the explanation

of Lebadea (vid. Bouché-Leclercq, op. cit. iii. p. 332, quoting from "Schol. Luc. Dial. Mort." iii.); the shrine of the Cabiri near Thebes in Boeotia gave way to a Christian Church; the shrine of the temple of the Muses on Mt. Helicon was removed for a church of Hagia Triada (Holy Trinity); (vid. Frazer, "Comm. Paus." ix. 25, 5; 29, 5). So, too, in Ireland, according to tradition, St. Patrick consecrated the pagan shrines to Christian usage.

[1] Cf. Il. ἐν ἠγαθέῃ, Od. viii. 80; Hes. Th. 499, etc.

[2] For the Hyperboreans vid. Farnell, op. cit. iv. p. 100 ff.; Bouché-Leclercq, op. cit. iii. p. 16 ff.; K. O. Müller, "Dorians," i. p. 294 ff.

[3] Cf. Pind. O. iii. 31-2, P. x. 29 ff. Cf. τύχη ὑπερβόρεος, a proverb for more than human happiness, vid. Aesch. Cho. 373.

[4] O. iii. 31.   [5] iv. 36.

The Influence of the Apolline Oracle

of Ahrens is largely accepted by scholars. According to him the form Ὑπερβόρεοι is merely a lengthening, due to false popular etymology, of Ὑπέρβοροι, which equals Ὑπέρφοροι,[1] a possible variant of Ὑπερφέρεται,[2] i.e. the sacred ministers who carry the cereal offerings from one community to another, and whom Herodotus calls Περφερέες.[3] We are told in Herodotus[4] that even in the writer's own time certain cereal offerings[5] came to Delos for the early summer festival of Apollo, arriving by a circuitous route (which he believed started with the Hyperboreans), and accompanied by sacred carriers, called Περφερέες.

As the name can be traced back to the eighth century B.C.,[6] it would appear that in the earliest times certain settlements of Greeks on the most northern boundary of Hellas[7] were accustomed to

---

[1] β being = φ in Northern Greek. Cf. Βερενίκη for Φερενίκη.

[2] From this word would be derived the Macedonian month Ὑπερβερεταῖος.

[3] iv. 36.　　　　　　　　　　　　[4] iv. 33.

[5] H. speaks of them merely as " sacred things wrapped in straw," but Callim. Hymn. Del. 284, speaks more expressly of them as καλάμην καὶ ἱερὰ δράγματα, " straw and the sacred corn-stalks."

[6] Hdt. iv. 32, says that the Hyperborei were mentioned by Hesiod and by the epic poet of the Epigoni (ἀλλ' Ἡσιόδῳ μέν ἐστι περὶ Ὑπερβορέων εἰρημένα, ἔστι δὲ καὶ Ὁμήρῳ ἐν Ἐπιγόνοισι). The writer of Hom. Hymn. Bacch. 29, refers to them.

[7] Hyperborean names we meet with, Pagasus, Aguieus (Paus. x. 5. 8), Orpis, Hecaerge, Loxo ("Et. Mag." p. 461, 55), Hyperoche and Laodice (Hdt. iv. 33, Euseb. Pr. Ev. ii. 6. 4, quoting Clem. Alex. Protrept.) are all Greek. Alcaeus

43

The Delphic Oracle

send first-fruits for the god to some famous cult-centre in the south. But this cult-centre must have been originally not Delos but Delphi, for while the latter is known and flourishing in the days of Homer the former is as yet obscure. Now there are many points of association of Delphi with the Hyperboreans. Its most ancient temple was of laurel wood, built by Hyperborean architects, Pagasus and Aguieus.[1] The poem of Alcaeus,[2] paraphrased by Himerius, speaks of Apollo's return to Delphi at mid-summer from the land of the Hyperboreans. The Oracle of the god was instituted by Olen (" Apollo's first interpreter ") and others arriving from the Hyperboreans.[3] Delphi, then, was the ancient shrine to which pilgrims from the distant North brought first-fruits to Apollo—a fact which, too, must have heightened the idea of sanctity and

(Hymn. Ap. apud Him. Or. xiv.) regarded them as living in the north of Greece, probably around Tempe. Serv. Aen. ii. 858 (quoted by Farnell, op. cit. iv. p. 418), assigned them to Thrace.

[1] Paus. x. 5. 8 :

> ἔνθα τοι εὔμνηστον χρηστήριον ἐκτέλεσαντο
> παῖδες Ὑπερβορέων Παγασὸς καὶ δῖος Ἀγυιεύς.

Vid. ibid. x. 5. 9 : ποιηθῆναι δὲ τὸν ναὸν τῷ Ἀπόλλωνι τὸ ἀρχαιότατον δάφνης φασί.

[2] Bergk, "Lyr. Gr." p. 704.

[3] Paus. x. 5. 8 : ἐπαριθμοῦσα δὲ καὶ ἄλλους τῶν Ὑπερβορέων, ἐπὶ τελευτῇ τοῦ ὕμνου τὸν Ὠλῆνα ὠνόμασεν (sc. ἡ Βοίω)·

> " Ὠλήν θ' ὃς γένετο πρῶτος Φοίβοιο προφάτας,
> πρῶτος δ' ἀρχαίων ἐπέων τεκτάνατ' ἀοιδάν."

44

antiquity, wherewith the Greeks invested their great central sanctuary.

Another circumstance, which must have contributed to the prestige of the Apolline Oracle at Delphi, is the fact of Apollo's association there with Zeus not indeed in cult—for Zeus had no cult as such at Delphi[1]—but in literature. Now Apollo is said to be the "interpreter," the "mouth-piece," of his father;[2] now his prophecy is declared to be "the sweetly-speaking message of Zeus,"[3] now he is said to have been "purified in Tempe by the plans of Zeus that excelleth."[4] The poets have created for him the epithets Ζηνόφρων[5] and Ζηνοδότηρ. They constantly declare that every word that falls from the tripod is inspired by Zeus himself.[6] He

[1] Cf. Farnell, op. cit. iv. p. 233, note.

[2] Aesch. Eum. 19, Διὸς προφήτης δ' ἐστι Λοξίας πατρός. προφήτης ="interpreter," not prophet; cf. Pind. N. 1, 91, Διὸς προφάταν (Tiresias); Hom. Hymn. Herm. 532; Plat. Tim. 72 B, who dist. μάντις, "inspired seer," from προφήτης, "interpreter of oracles"; Eur. Ion, 416, τίς προφητεύει θεοῦ; "who is spokesman of the god?"

[3] Soph. O.T. 151, ὦ Διὸς ἁδυεπὲς φάτι.

[4] Paean of Ariston. (B.C.H. xvii. pp. 561 ff.), 7–8 βουλαῖς Ζηνὸς ὑπειρόχου; cf. New Hymn to Ap. (B.C.H. xviii. p. 352), 19. To this association of Ap. with Zeus at Delphi A. Lang (Hom. Hymns, Trans., Introd. pp. 30–31) shows some interesting parallels in present-day savage myth. In America, he says, in the Andaman Islands and in Australia, subordinate to the primal being, there exists another who enters into much closer relations with mankind, and who is concerned with healing and prophecy.

[5] Vid. L. and S., s.v. Ζηνόφρων, quoting "Anth. Pal.," p. 9, 525, 7.

[6] Aesch. Eum. 615–18.

The Delphic Oracle

is the sole confidant of his father : he alone must know the mind of " the ruler of gods and men." [1] And so it came about that every rival institution outside the sphere of Apolline influence was reduced to a second-rate importance. Even the great Homeric diviners, Calchas [2] and Helenus, [3] have received their prophecy and prestige from Apollo.

Next come what may be termed the geographical causes [4] of the influence of the Apolline Oracle. These are twofold. In the first place, there was the extraordinary natural impressiveness of the surroundings, which tended to lift up men's minds and hearts to commune with God. The wild and rugged beauty of the scene ; the towering summit [5]

[1] Hom. Hymn. Merc. 535 ff. Apollo, however, though the confidant of Zeus, is never the dispenser of Fate ; Zeus alone is Μοιραγέτης. The only case in literature and cult where Apollo has this title is that in Paus. x. 24. 4, where we are told that in the temple at Delphi there stood an image of Zeus Μοιραγέτης and Ap. Μοιραγέτης. Here Apollo seems to have but temporarily borrowed the title from his father. Cf. Farnell, op. cit. iv. p. 233.

[2] Il. i. 72. . . . διὰ μαντοσύνην, τήν οἱ πόρε Φοῖβος 'Απόλλων.

[3] Il. vii. 44. Cf. Cassandra (Aesch. Ag. 1202 ; Verg. Aen. ii. 343).

[4] For the Delphic topography vid. Strab. 418 ; Paus. x. 8. 8–9 ; Hom. Hymn. Ap. 282–85 ; Just. xxiv. 6. Among modern writers vid. P.W. s.v. Delphoi, 2517 (Philippson) ; Frazer, " Comm. Paus." x. 5. 5, 8. 5 ; Foucart, " Mém. sur Delph." p. 1 ff. ; Mahaffy, " Rambles and Studies in Greece " (1907), pp. 243 ff. ; Baedeker, " Greece " ('09), pp. 141–2 ; Bouché-Leclercq, op. cit. iii. pp. 42–3.

[5] This was known as Λυκώρεια (modern Liakoura), standing about 8,000 ft. above sea-level.

The Influence of the Apolline Oracle

of snow-clad [1] Parnassus ; the dark and mysterious gorge between the glittering Phaedriades ; [2] the streams [3] of mysterious sources issuing from the very rocks ; the sonorous echoes reverberating from the sides of the cliffs ; the frequent earth-shocks ; the sudden alternations of brilliant sunshine and dark shadow—all these features were singularly calculated to strike the superstitious minds of bygone ages. Even now the whole place seems redolent of mystery, and can evoke under favourable conditions certain feelings of enthusiasm not unlike the ancient spirit of prophecy. Even the modern traveller is struck by this scene of stern and awful majesty, and comes to the conclusion that no other spot perhaps in Europe was so formed by nature to work upon the religious

[1] Cf. νιφόεντα, Hom. Hymn. Ap. 282 ; νιφόβολος, Eur. Phoen. 206 ; ἀκρονιφής, Fr. Delph. Hymn, *B.C.H.* xviii. p. 282.

[2] These were great steep cliffs above Delphi, being called Φαιδριάδες, " gleaming " (from φαιδρός), because of their splendour in the morning sunshine (vid. Eur. Ion, 86 ff.). They culminated in two lofty peaks (rising about 2,000 ft. above sea-level), the easternmost of which was known as 'Τάμπεια, the westernmost perhaps as Ναυπλία. They are frequently referred to by the poets, cf. δικόρυφος πλάξ, Eur. Bacch. 307 (πλάξ referring to the uplands stretching between these lower peaks and Parnassus) ; ὑπὲρ διλόφου πέτρας κ.τ.λ., Soph. Ant. 1125. The Roman poets apparently confounded these peaks with Parnassus itself. Cf. Lucan (Phars. v. 72), " Parnassus gemino petit aethera colle."

[3] These fountains were three in number, Castalia, Cassotis, Delphousa. They remain unchanged to the present day, being still a distinctive feature in the site of the ancient oracle. Vid. Mahaffy, " Rambles and Studies in Greece," pp. 243–4.

The Delphic Oracle

temperament, and that for the ancients it was supremely fitted for the utterance of the oracles of the gods.

Again, if we look at the map, we see at once that Delphi, secluded as it was, had certain geographical advantages of position. It was the most convenient centre for all the leading Greek communities. It was easily approached by two paths from north and east, while from the Peloponnesus the states and cities of the Isthmus had an easy access by the Gulf of Corinth. Little wonder is it, then, that Delphi was regarded as the " navel of the earth " (ὁ τῆς γῆς ὀμφαλός [1]).

[1] All are familiar with the legend of the two eagles sent out by Zeus from opposite extremities of the earth and meeting at Delphi. Hence Delphi was called ὁ τῆς γῆς ὀμφαλός, " the navel of the earth," and a conical stone—the famous ὀμφαλός, regarding which there has been so much controversy in ancient and modern times—was supposed to mark the spot where they met as centre of the earth. (For refs. to the ὀμφαλός vid. Schol. Pind. P. 4. 6 ff.; Aesch. Eum. 39 ff.; Varro, De Lingua Lat. 7, 17; Strab. p. 119; Schol. Lucian, De Saltat. 38; Paus. x. 16. 3, with Frazer's "Comm."; Plat. Rep. 427C). It is interesting to note that most peoples believed that they possessed " the navel of the earth." In Ireland it was supposed to be in Meath (Old Irish Medio-n). The central point was the hill of Uisnech, now Ushriagh Hill, in Co. Westmeath. The Omphalos was symbolized by a stone which still exists. Giraldus Cambrensis (in " Topogr. Hib.") says that this stone was called " Umbilicus Hiberniae." According to a text of the eleventh or twelfth century A.D. it seems there was an important oracle situated beside Uisnech. So, too, in Gaul the Omphalos was supposed to lie in the country of the Carnutes. (Cf. M. J. Loth in " Comptes Rendus, 1914," pp. 182, 481.)

48

The Influence of the Delphic Oracle

We now come to the intrinsic causes of the great prestige of the Delphic Oracle. First among these causes should be placed the creation at Delphi of an enthusiastic mantic. This last expression needs some explanation. The ancient Greeks and Romans recognized two principal methods of divination, the one intuitive or natural (ἄτεχνος, ἀδίδακτος), the other inductive or artificial (ἔντεχνος, τεχνική, artificiosa).[1] The former consisted in a certain divine madness or ecstasy, in which the human soul is possessed by the divinity (μαντικὴ ἔνθεος),[2] and while under this inspiration shows itself possessed of superhuman knowledge. The other method of divination was, on the contrary, a sane and rational procedure, derived from the observation of certain signs, such as the flight or cry of birds,[3] but based,

[1] Modern writers generally follow Bouché-Leclercq, op. cit. i. pp. 107, 114, 174, 273-4, in the classification of mantic methods. His classification, however, is not new: it merely repeats that of Cic. De Div. i. 6, "duo sunt enim divinandi genera, quorum alterum artis est, alterum naturae" (which statement Cic. explains, ibid. i. 18, § 34, ii. 11, §§ 26-7); cf. Plat. Phaedr. p. 244B, where the two methods are defined: ἡ μαντικὴ ἔνθεος, and ἡ τῶν ἐμφρόνων ζήτησις τοῦ μέλλοντος διά τε ὀρνίθων ποιουμένη καὶ τῶν ἄλλων σημείων.

[2] Plat. l.c. The words μάντις, μαντική, etc., all come from √MAN, which appears in μαίνομαι, mens. Cf. Plat. Tim. 72B; Cic. De Div. i. 1, § 1, 18, § 34; vid. Giles, "Comp. Phil." §§ 25-26. With μαντικὴ ἔνθεος cf. ἔνθεος τέχνης, "gifted by Heaven with prophetic art," Aesch. Eum. 17.

[3] Omens from birds were included under the general term ὀρνιθομαντεία, vid. Bouché-Leclercq, op. cit. i. p. 127 ff. Cf. Lat. auspicium and augurium. So important a rôle did birds

The Delphic Oracle

however, upon some primordial revelation. The first method was indeed the higher kind of prophecy, but the second was apparently the older, for it belonged to all the great seers of the heroic age, such as Calchas, Helenus, and Tiresias, who always read the future in prodigies, or external signs. Indeed, a third method of divination might be added to the above—though not at all so common— oneiromancy, or divination by dreams, particularly under the form of " incubation " [1] (ἐγκοίμησις), as it was called. This method was usually connected with the chthonian divinities and heroes, and we have seen that it was once in vogue at Delphi, when the cult of Ge there flourished. So much by way of preliminary.

The first method mentioned above—the intuitive or natural—was constantly associated at Delphi with Apollo : the prophetic frenzy of the Pythia, like that of Cassandra [2] of old, was regarded as coming directly from the god. To this fact beyond all others must be attributed the peculiar influence of the Delphic Oracle of Apollo. That a mortal

play in divination that the Greek word for " omen," οἰωνός, originally meant " bird." For οἰωνός as " bird " vid. Aesch. Ag. 115, as " omen " vid. Il. xii. 243, εἰς οἰωνὸς ἄριστος κ.τ.λ. For the observance of omens from birds as a *sine qua non* for obtaining a true response at Delphi vid. Hom. Hymn. Merc. 543–47.

[1] Vid. supr. p. 7.

[2] For her magnificent outburst of prophetic frenzy vid. Aesch. Ag. 1072 ff. Cf. Cic. De Div. i. 31, § 67, " deus inclusus corpore humano, iam non Cassandra, loquitur."

should be visibly possessed by the divinity, who moulds his accents and speaks with his voice is truly an awe-inspiring phenomenon,[1] and has been at all times and in all religions the highest and most impressive form of prophecy.

Was the second method—the inductive or artificial—ever in vogue at Delphi in connexion with the Apolline cult ? According to Rohde,[2] the original Apolline method of divination was of this type, and the enthusiastic style was the product of a later age, when Dionysus was almost on an equal footing with Apollo at Delphi, and the Pythia shared to some extent the character of the Maenad. This theory has its strong points : at Delphi there were certainly other methods of divination than the ecstatic. Eponymous heroes, Delphus[3] and Parnassus,[4] were spoken of as inventors of arts of soothsaying through the inspection of entrails and the flight of birds. The word ἀναιρεῖν,[5] commonly used in reference to the Pythia's response, seems to point to a method of divination by lot at Delphi [6]

[1] According to Paus. i. 34, ecstatic inspiration was connected first with the Apolline oracles.

[2] " Psyche " (pp. 56–61), quoted by Farnell, op. cit. iv. p. 190.

[3] Plin. vii. 56, 203.

[4] Paus. x. 6. 1.

[5] Cf. ἀνεῖλεν ἡ· Πυθίη κ.τ.λ., Hdt. i. 13, etc.

[6] Cf. Hom. Hymn. Merc. 552–63, where the " three sisters " (from whom Her. is recommended by Apollo to learn the prophetic art) are to be identified with the Θριαί, who are but the mythological explanation of the θριαί, or divining pebbles. Cf. Zenob. Prov. Cent. v. 75, Φιλόχορός φησιν ὅτι νύμφαι κατεῖχον

The Delphic Oracle

(ἡ διὰ ψήφων μαντική). Indeed, Suidas [1] tells us that " divining pebbles " (μαντικαὶ ψῆφοι) lay in some receptacle above the tripod. The word ἀναιρεῖν, then, probably meant the " taking up " of the divining pebbles. But what does all this prove ? It merely shows that the enthusiastic method was not the only one possible at Delphi, but does not at all affirm that the enthusiastic method was alien to Apollo's proper style. So there is no need of introducing Dionysus as a *deus ex machina*.

At Delphi the medium of divine inspiration was always a woman, the rule being maintained, with possibly one exception,[2] throughout the whole Apolline period. The Pythia must be a freeborn Delphian,[3] but otherwise no condition of birth or rank or culture was obligatory. All that was required was that " she have spent her life in a virtuous manner " [4] and continue to live ritualistically pure. It is clear from Plutarch,[5] that whatever she may have been under the influence of inspiration, ordinarily she was not a very striking personage, being but a simple, unlettered peasant

τὸν Πάρνασσον . . . καλούμεναι Θριαί, ἀφ' ὧν αἱ μαντικαὶ ψῆφοι θριαὶ καλοῦνται (vid. Sikes and Allen, Hom. Hymns, App. III.).

[1] s.v. Πυθώ (quoted by Farnell, op. cit. iv. p. 386).

[2] Cf. Paus. x. 5. 7, who says that Boeo, a woman of the country, in a hymn composed for the Delphians, declared that Olen was the first to give oracles and sing in hexameters, and that he was the " first prophet of Phoebus." Vid. supr. p. 44.

[3] Plut. De Pyth. Orac. xxii. ; Eur. Ion, 1323.

[4] Plut. De Pyth. Orac. xxii., De Def. Orac. li.

[5] De Pyth. Orac. xxii.

The Influence of the Delphic Oracle

woman, " having acquired nothing from art or training or help of any sort." Originally virginity [1] was a necessary condition for holding the office, but as youthful virginity proved dangerous on at least one occasion,[2] it was ordained by the Delphians that in future a married woman of over fifty years should give the öracles.[3] She should, however, be still attired as a maiden [4] by way of recollection of the ancient custom. The rule of virginity, however, seems to have been revived in Plutarch's time.[5] In early times there was but one Pythia. Later on, however, " when Greece was strong in cities and the place was thronged with people," two were appointed (one apparently being unable to stand the strain), whilst a third was appointed as assistant to them.[6] Later still, in Plutarch's day, one Pythia sufficed for the diminished clientèle of the Oracle.[7] The Pythia, before taking her seat upon the oracular tripod, had to prepare herself for the solemn act by certain ritualistic observances. She began her

---

[1] Virginity being regarded as more in consonance with the Pythia's relations with the bright, pure Apollo. Cf. Diod. xvi. 26, 6, διὰ τὸ τῆς φύσεως ἀδιάφθορον κ.τ.λ.

[2] Diod. l. c.

[3] Diod. l. c.

[4] Diod. l. c., κοσμεῖσθαι δ' αὐτὴν παρθενικῇ σκευῇ κ.τ.λ. Cf. Aesch. Eum. 38, γραῦς ἀντίπαις.

[5] Cf. De Def. Orac. xlvi. διαφυλάττοντας (τὴν Πυθίαν) ἁγνὴν διὰ βίου καὶ καθαρεύουσαν ; ibid. li., καὶ συνουσίας ἁγνὸν τὸ σῶμα καὶ τὸν βίον ὅλως ἀνεπίμικτον ἀλλοδαπαῖς ὁμιλίαις καὶ ἄθικτον φυλάττουσι τῆς Πυθιάδος.

[6] Plut. De Def. Orac. viii.　　　　[7] Plut. ibid.

53

The Delphic Oracle

preparation by fasting and bathing in the Castalian spring.[1] If the omens were favourable,[2] the Pythia first chewed the leaves of the sacred laurel,[3] drank from the water of the spring Cassotis,[3] and burned laurel leaves and barley meal [4] (and perhaps myrrh) [5] in " the never-dying fire " [6] on the altar of the god. All this, however, was but preparatory to the great moment when she mounted the tripod (which was placed directly over the chasm), and, filled with the

[1] Schol. Eur. Phoen. 223 (vid. Bouché-Leclercq, op. cit. iii. p. 100). Bathing in the Castalian fountain before they entered the temple was incumbent on the ministers of Apollo, vid. Eur. Ion, 94–7. The fountain and bath still remain, vid. Baed. " Greece," pp. 149-50 ; Mahaffy, " Rambles and Studies in Greece," p. 238.

[2] For the omens taken from the manner in which bulls and he-goats ate—or didn't eat—certain foods, and from the cold water test in case of goats, vid. Plut. De Def. Orac. xlix.

[3] Lucian, Bis. Acc. i., μασησαμένη τῆς δάφνης ; Tzet. Schol. Lycophr. vi. (quoted by Frazer, " Comm. Paus." x. 5. 5). Cf. F. W. H. Myers, " Essays," p. 65. That the Pythia drank from the water of the sacred spring is suggested by the words of the oracle supposed to have been delivered to Julian : ἀπέσβετο καὶ λάλον ὕδωρ (vid. infr. p. 180). Cf. σεσίγηται γοῦν ἡ Κασταλίας πηγὴ, καὶ Κολοφῶνος ἄλλη πηγὴ, καὶ τὰ ἄλλα ὁμοίως τέθνηκε νάματα μαντικά, Euseb. Pr. Ev. ii. 3, 2 (quoting Clem. Alex. Protrep.). Paus. (x. 24. 7) says that the water of the spring Cassotis made the Delphic women prophetic, vid. infr. p. 57, n. 5.

[4] Plut. De Pyth. Orac. vi. ; De E apud Delph. ii.

[5] Eur. Ion, 89–90, σμύρνης δ' ἀνύδρου καπνὸς εἰς ὀρόφους | Φοίβου πέτεται. This would probably account for the " sweet odour " (εὐωδία) which sometimes pervaded the oracular chamber (vid. Plut. De Def. Orac. 50).

[6] ἐπὶ τοῦ πυρὸς τοῦ ἀθανάτου, Plut. De E apud Delph. ii. Cf. Aesch. Cho. 1037.

The Influence of the Delphic Oracle

divine *afflatus*, burst forth into wild prophetic utterance.[1] These frenzied, incoherent cries were, however, taken down and interpreted, according to some conventional code, by the προφήτης,[2] who was in attendance.

Why was a woman chosen as the organ of inspiration at Delphi ? In the first place, it is quite possible that the Pythia was a heritage from the primal cult of Ge. Just as the Nature-goddess of Crete in all probability had an orgiastic and ecstatic worship [3] in the earliest times, and Dodona on the testimony of Plato [4] had its inspired priestesses, so too, probably, the Earth-goddess of Pytho had an ecstatic cult, of which the Pythia was a survival. But more fundamental is the psychological reason. It has been observed at all times and in all countries that women are especially prone to orgiastic religious seizure, and with such moods

[1] The *locus classicus* for the description of the Pythian frenzy is Lucan, Phars. v. 161 ff. The picture, however, seems overdrawn. Probably the poet is drawing on the statements of others and his own imagination rather than on first-hand information.

[2] For the προφήτης vid. App. B.

[3] On a seal-design found in the palace of Cnossus the goddess was represented amid rock scenery with a female figure seemingly engaged at an orgiastic dance. Vid. Farnell (quoting Evans), op. cit. iii. p. 297.

[4] Phaedr. p. 244B, ἥ τε γὰρ δὴ ἐν Δελφοῖς προφῆτις, αἵ τε ἐν Δωδώνῃ ἱέρειαι μανεῖσαι μὲν πολλὰ δὴ καὶ καλὰ ἰδίᾳ τε καὶ δημοσίᾳ τὴν Ἑλλάδα εἰργάσαντο κ.τ.λ. Cf. Philostr. Apollon. of Tyana, iii. 42, οἱ μαντικῇ . . . χαίροντες . . . θεοί τε ὑπ αὐτῆς γίγνονται καὶ πρὸς σωτηρίαν ἀνθρώπων πράττουσι.

The Delphic Oracle

prophecy and magic have been associated. And so it is to-day. The Shamaness is thought as a rule more powerful in magic than the Shaman : [1] she is supposed to possess more " mana." [2] Among the tribes of Hindoo Koosh, near Gilgit, the Dainyals, or diviners, are generally women, [3] who, not unlike the Pythia of old, work themselves into a prophetic frenzy by inhaling the fumes of burning cedar-wood, their sacred tree. So, too, the modern spiritistic medium is generally a woman, [4] and, exactly as in the case of the Pythia, chosen from among the uneducated classes, the psychological ground being, of course, that the minds of simple, uneducated folk are more plastic and more readily influenced by " spiritual " forces. The person chosen as Pythia, however, does not seem to have been of specially susceptible temperament, such as a neurotic or hysterical subject. Indeed the contrary seems true—that only a woman of well-balanced temperament was chosen for the office.

[1] Shaman is the title of the Siberian wizards, who seek to procure by agitated trance manifestations from their gods.

[2] The Melanesian word " mana " is now generally used to designate the power which gives efficacy to the magic act.

[3] Vid. Frazer, " Comm. Paus." x. 5. 5.

[4] Vid. McKenzie, " Spirit Intercourse," p. 14. The same writer (pp. 51–2, 142–4) gives the preparations necessary on the part of the spiritistic medium for successful spirit intercourse, which are strangely reminiscent of those enjoined on the Pythia. Indeed, there is an extraordinary parallelism between modern spiritistic teaching and the doctrine of spirit communication given by Porphyry (ap. Euseb. Pr. Ev. iv. 1, 5 ; v. 8, 9, 12 ; vi. 5), and Proclus (quoted by Myers, " Essays," pp. 83–4).

The Influence of the Delphic Oracle

For Plutarch tells us that the Pythia before ascending the tripod should have her soul free from perturbation,[1] and that, " when she has departed from the tripod and the inspiration is past, she continues in calm and peace." [2]

We now come to the important but very difficult question of the *cause* of the Delphic inspiration. Among ancient writers later authorities at least are agreed that a physical cause co-operated, or even was the leading agency, in the Pythian frenzy. This physical cause was a certain exhalation,[3] a mephitic gas ascending from the chasm or fissure in the earth [4] over which the prophetic tripod was placed. Such is the view of Pausanias [5] and more

[1] Vid. De Def. Orac. 1. ; cf. Cic. De Div. i. 38, § 81, "animi enim integri, non vitiosi est corporis divinatio."

[2] Vid. Amatorius, xv.

[3] The ancient writers speak variously of it as a " breath " (πνεῦμα, *spiritus*, *anhelitus*), " vapour " (ἀτμός), " exhalation " (ἀναθυμίασις). Vid. Plut. De Def. Orac. xlvi. (where all three are mentioned together) ; Strab. 419 C ; Lucan, Phars. v. 132 ; Cic. De Div. ii. 57, § 117.

[4] χάσμα γῆς, στόμιον, *fauces*.

[5] x. 5. 7, ἤκουσα δὲ καὶ ὡς ἄνδρες ποιμαίνοντες ἐπιτύχοιεν τῷ μαντείῳ, καὶ ἔνθεοι ἐγένοντο ὑπὸ τοῦ ἀτμοῦ καὶ ἐμαντεύσαντο ἐξ Ἀπόλλωνος. Afterwards, however (x. 24. 7), he says that it is the water of the fountain Cassotis, flowing through the chasm, that makes the women prophetic. Cf. Ov. (Am. i. 15, 35–6), who attributes inspiring power to the water of the fountain Castalia : " mihi flavus Apollo | pocula Castaliae plena ministret aquae."

The Italians connected brooks with the gift of prophecy. Vid. Ov. Fasti, iii. 298–9). Cf. σεσίγηται γοῦν ἡ Κασταλίας πηγή, κ.τ.λ. (Euseb. Pr. Ev. ii. 3. 2, quoting Clem. Alex. Protrept., cited supr. p. 54, n. 3).

The Delphic Oracle

explicitly still of Strabo.[1] Plutarch,[2] too, whose observations on the matter should be of the highest worth, inasmuch as he was a clear-headed, well-educated man, not at all prone to superstition,[3] and having ample opportunity of detecting any fraud or juggling on the part of the Delphic priesthood—Plutarch is a firm believer that the prophetic frenzy was caused by this vapour. The vapour, however (he goes on to explain), is but a mere instrument : the final cause of the power which the vapour possesses is the Deity. The earth breeds these prophetic exhalations. He who imparts the faculty for " tempering and changing " the souls of men to prophetic power is the Sun,[4] with whom Plutarch constantly identifies Apollo. There is, however, a third factor in the process—the " demons," " intermediate between gods and men," who are " presidents and ministers and guardians " of this " tempering," now increasing, now diminishing the ecstatic power.[5]

[1] 419 C: φασὶ δ᾽ εἶναι τὸ μαντεῖον ἄντρον κοῖλον κατὰ βάθους οὐ εὐρύστομον, ἀναφέρεσθαι δ᾽ ἐξ αὐτοῦ πνεῦμα ἐνθουσιαστικὸν, ὑπερκεῖσθαι δὲ τοῦ στομίου τρίποδα ὑψηλὸν ἐφ᾽ ὃν τὴν Πυθίαν ἀναβαίνουσαν δεχομένην τὸ πνεῦμα ἀποθεσπίζειν ἔμμετρα καὶ ἄμμετρα. Cf. Diod. xvi. 26 ; Cic. De Div. ii. 57, §§ 117–8 ; Lucan, Phars. v. 132–3, " . . . seu spiritus istas destituit fauces," etc., and ibid. 83–4, " . . . ventosque loquaces exhalare solum," also ibid. 164–5.

[2] De Def. Orac. xxxviii. to end. Vid. esp. xliii.

[3] Vid. Plut. De Superstit.

[4] De Def. Orac. xlviii. : ὁ δὲ πᾶσαν ἐνδιδοὺς κράσεως τῇ γῇ καὶ μεταβολῆς δύναμιν ἥλιος, κ.τ.λ.

[5] Ibid. xxxviii. xlviii.

The Influence of the Delphic Oracle

All this, however, raises two difficulties, the one geological, the other literary. Let us take first the geological difficulty. The recent French excavations have laid bare the foundations and floor of the fourth-century temple,[1] but no trace whatever could be found of the famous cleft. Hence some have concluded that the stories about the mephitic exhalations were mere figments of the imagination, for there never existed such a cleft at all. The simple answer to the difficulty is that earthquakes, which, as has been shown, were so prevalent at Delphi, have long since obliterated all traces of the cleft. The same must be said of the " cave "[2] which the ancient writers refer to as having been the oracular shrine proper. The French excavators could find no trace of any cave or large subterranean chamber.[3] It, too, vanished in the changes

---

[1] After its destruction by fire in 548 B.C. the temple was rebuilt twice, viz. in the sixth and fourth centuries B.C. It was repaired—some think actually rebuilt—by Nero and Domitian in the first century A.D. (vid. infr. pp. 176–78). For a history of the temple vid. Frazer, " Comm. Paus." v. pp. 328–40 ; Homolle, *B.C.H.* xx. p. 641 ff.

[2] Cf. Strab. 419 C. Certainly that the oracular shrine proper was below the level of the temple is clear from the statements which represent the priestess as *going down* to consult the Oracle. Cf. Plut. De Def. Orac. li. ; De Pyth. Orac. vi. xxii. xxviii.

[3] Vid. *B.C.H.* xviii. p. 93 ff. Regarding the subterranean galleries which Foucart and Pomtow thought they had discovered, these proved on excavation to be either narrow corridors or else small chambers, in height not more than about 6½ ft. They are very numerous, but it is doubtful if they were

The Delphic Oracle

which earth-shocks wrought in the site of Delphi. It is highly probable, then, that there was a small cleft or crack in the earth or floor of the temple, through which a slight draught of air might sometimes be felt.[1] The expression in Aeschylus,[2] ὦ μέγα ναίων στόμιον, naturally refers to Apollo (not Hades), who is regarded as indwelling in the oracular chasm.

Let us now turn to the literary difficulty. The idea that the Delphic inspiration was due to a mephitic vapour rests wholly on the authority of later writers: the early writers are absolutely silent on the matter. There is never a word about this exhalation in the descriptions of the shrine which Aeschylus and Euripides have given us. Both of these beyond all doubt believed that an influence causing prophetic frenzy did ascend from the Delphic chasm. But the *materializing* of that influence, so as to make it definitely sensuous,

---

ever utilized as vaults, for no important object was found in them. Vid. *B.C.H.* xviii. p. 775 ff.

[1] This is practically what is stated by Just. (xxiv. 6). According to him " a cold air " was forcibly expelled upwards from a hole in the ground, which turned the minds of the prophetesses to madness (" . . . profundum terrae foramen, quod in oracula patet : ex quo frigidus spiritus, vi quadam velut vento in sublime expulsus, mentes vatum in vecordiam vertit "). Cf. Lucan, Phars. v. 83–4, " ventosque loquaces exhalare solum." Cf. Cic. De Div. ii. 117, who calls the exhalation " anhelitus terrae " and " afflatus e terra." Cic., however, seems to doubt its existence at all, for he says (ibid. 118) " si unquam fuisset."

[2] Cho. 806-7.

was the work of writers of a later day. Their exaggerations would be amply accounted for by the supposition already made—that there was a small cleft in the earth, through which occasionally a slight draught of air was felt.

This question of the cause of the Delphic inspiration raises another very important, but extremely difficult question—a question but too often ignored : was the Delphic Oracle genuine, or was it a mere sham, a conscious fraud, at least on the part of the ministers, trading on the credulity of an uncritical and superstitious age ? An institution which for ages [1] maintained its credit more or less unimpaired, whose origin was lost in the twilight of antiquity, and whose career extended well into Christian times ; an institution which numbered among its clientèle men of the highest intellects as well as those of simple, unquestioning faith—surely such an institution would seem to claim some better foundation than mere fraud ? Certainly we find the voice of antiquity proclaiming the veracity of the Oracle. In magnificent lines Pindar asserts the omniscience of Apollo, who " knows the end supreme of all things, and all the ways that lead thereto ; the number of the leaves that the earth putteth forth in spring ; the number of the sands that in the sea and the rivers are driven before the waves

[1] Plut. De Pyth. Orac. xxix. speaks of the " 3,000 years old reputation " of the Oracle (. . . δεδιότες μὴ τρισχιλίων ἐτῶν ἀποβάλῃ δόξαν ὁ τόπος).

The Delphic Oracle

and the rushing winds; that which is to be, and whence it is to come." [1] And this omniscience is coupled with veracity, for Apollo " can have nothing to do with falsehood." [2] Similar is the testimony of Aeschylus.[3] Aye, even Euripides, " the rationalist," at times asserts his faith in Apollo's oracular powers, declaring that he " alone should prophesy unto men " [4]—though indeed to many statements like that in the *Ion* [5] seem a contradiction of this.

More important still is the testimony of the ancient philosophers. Socrates was a firm believer in the Delphic Oracle, which declared him " the

[1] P. ix. 45–9. These lines remind us of the sublime exordium of the oracle given to Croesus (Hdt. i. 47) :

οἶδα δ' ἐγὼ ψάμμου τ' ἀριθμόν, καὶ μέτρα θαλάσσης,
καὶ κωφοῦ συνίημι, καὶ οὐ φωνεῦντος ἀκούω—

words which evidently impressed the Greeks, for the Delphians had them inscribed upon a marble slab. This slab was found by Cyriac of Ancona in the sixteenth century. (Vid. Foucart, " Mémoire sur Delph." p. 139). Philostr. Apollon. of Tyana, vi. 12, refers to them. Cf. also (for the expression of Apollo's omniscience) Hom. Hymn. Merc. 467, σὺ δὲ φρεσὶ πάντ' εὖ οἶδας; Lucan, Phars. v. 88–90, ". . . deus, omnia cursus | aeterni secreta tenens, mundique futuri | conscius."

[2] Pind. P. ix. 42, σέ, τὸν οὐ θεμιτὸν ψεύδει θιγεῖν.

[3] Eum. 615, μάντις ὢν δ' οὐ ψεύσομαι.

[4] Phoen. 958–9, Φοῖβον ἀνθρώποις μόνον | χρῆν θεσπιφδεῖν, κ.τ.λ.

[5] According to Verrall (vid. Introd. Ion) the play is but a skit on the Delphic Oracle. Certainly the statement (1537–8),

ὁ θεὸς ἀληθής, ἢ μάτην μαντεύεται,
ἐμοῦ ταράσσει, μῆτερ, εἰκότως φρένα,

seems to bear out Verrall's theory. It is possible of course that Euripides, while believing in Apollo in general, disbelieved in a particular shrine.

The Influence of the Delphic Oracle

wisest of all men," and from which he claimed
to have received a divine mission.[1]   Plato had
the highest respect for the Delphic god and his
office. " For the Delphian Apollo," he said, " there
will remain the most important, the noblest, and
the chiefest acts of legislation . . . the erection of
temples and the appointment of sacrifices and other
ceremonies connected with gods and demi-gods and
heroes. . . . For it is this god, I presume, expounding from his seat on the Omphalos at the earth's
centre, who is the national expositor to all men
on such matters." [2]   Most important of all is the
view of Plutarch, who, as we have seen, was constantly associated with the temple,[3] and thoroughly
understood its inner workings.   He had the highest
esteem for the Oracle, which had been the " author
of such great services to the Greeks in wars and
the founding of cities, on occasions of pestilence
and seasons of barrenness." [4]   " Never," he tri-
umphantly declared, " to the present day did the
language of the Pythia suffer any impeachment of
its veracity." [5]   Cicero, too, believed in the Oracle,
if we are to accept the statements regarding it

[1] Plat. Ap. v, xviii.   We see him advising Xenophon to
consult the Oracle (Xen. An. iii. 1, 5).

[2] Rep. 427 B–C.

[3] Plutarch held the priesthood at Delphi and passed his old
age there (vid. *P.W.* s.v. Delphoi, 2523 : " er lebte im Alter in D.
und bekleidete dort die Priesterwürde ").   He was ἐπιμελήτης of
the Amphictyonic Council in the reign of Hadrian (*C.I.G.* 1713).

[4] De Def. Orac. xlvi.

[5] De Pyth. Orac. xxix.

63

The Delphic Oracle

which he puts in the mouth of his brother Quintus in his treatise on Divination,[1] though he admits its diminished veracity and its consequent diminished glory in his own day. He himself consulted it, characteristically inquiring " how he should become most famous." The Pythia's answer was that " he should make his own nature, not the opinion of the many his guide in life "[2]—words of wisdom which the timid statesman would have done well to lay to heart.

In obedience to the Delphic Oracle the great rhetorician and sophist, Dio Chrysostom, wandered in beggar's disguise through many lands. " Do as thou dost," said Apollo to him, " until thou reach the end of the earth."[3]

[1] Vid. De Div. i. 19, § 37, "nunquam illud oraclum Delphis tam celebre et tam clarum fuisset neque tantis donis refertum omnium populorum atque regum, nisi omnis aetas oraclorum illorum veritatem esset experta"; ibid. § 38, "ut igitur nunc in minore gloria est, quia minus oraculorum veritas excellit, sic tum nisi summa veritate in tanta gloria non fuisset ; . . . modo id maneat quod negari non potest nisi omnem historiam perverterimus, multis saeclis verax fuisse id oraclum." Contrast, however, " . . . iam ut nihil possit esse contemptius " (De Div. ii. 57, § 117). Vid. infr. p. 175.

[2] Plut. Cic. v. προσέταξεν ἡ Πυθία τὴν ἑαυτοῦ φύσιν, ἀλλὰ μὴ τὴν τῶν πολλῶν δόξαν, ἡγέμονα ποιεῖσθαι τοῦ βίου. With the ethical precept—so strongly inculcated by the Stoics—embodied in the response cf. " congruere naturae cumque ea convenienter vivere," Cic. Tusc. v. 28, 82 ; " congruenter naturae convenienterque vivere," ibid. Fin. iii. 7, 26, etc.

[3] Vid. Dio Chry., περὶ φυγῆς, p. 221 : ἐκέλευε γάρ με αὐτὸ τοῦτο πράττειν ἐν ᾧ εἰμι πάσῃ προθυμίᾳ ὡς καλήν τινα καὶ συμφέρουσαν πρᾶξιν, ἕως ἂν, ἔφη, ἐπὶ τὸ ἔσχατον ἀπέλθῃς τῆς γῆς.

64

The Influence of the Delphic Oracle

Occasionally, however, we hear a discordant note in the chorus of approbation. Euripides' attitude towards the Oracle is somewhat doubtful. For, though he declares that " Phoebus alone should prophesy unto men," [1] yet he makes one of his characters exclaim that " it troubles his soul whether the god be true or doth idly prophesy." [2] Furthermore, he makes Orestes accuse Apollo of " much folly " in his oracular utterances. [3] His famous indictment of the prophetic art in the *Helen* [4] cannot, however, be adduced in proof of his disapproval of the mantic methods of Delphi. For here he seems to condemn merely divination drawn from " flame of fire " or " cries of birds," which he declares " bring naught of aid to mortals." Eusebius [5] tells us that " all the followers of Aristotle, the Cynics and Epicureans, and all those who were of similar views, laughed to scorn the oracles that were noised abroad among the Greeks themselves." Aristotle narrates how Hegesippus consulted the oracle of Zeus at Olympia, and then went to Delphi and asked Apollo " whether the son was of the same opinion

---

[1] Phoen. 958–9. Vid. supr. p. 62.

[2] Ion, 1537–8. Vid. supr. p. 62.

[3] El. 971, ὦ Φοῖβε, πολλήν γ' ἀμαθίαν ἐθέσπισας.

[4] 745 ff.

[5] Pr. Ev. iv. 3. 14. According to Cic. De Div. i. 3. 5, all the most ancient philosophers, except Xenophanes of Colophon and Epicurus, approved of divination.

The Delphic Oracle

as the father." [1]   All are familiar with the scoffing
allusions of the sceptic Lucian, who depicts in
amusing fashion the god's lack of poetic skill in
the composition of his hexameters, and the an-
noyance to which he must be subjected when
he has to hurry from the most distant parts to
his oracular post, whenever the Pythia elects
" to chew the laurel-leaf and drink of the sacred
spring." [2]

Yet, on the whole, the voice of antiquity proclaimed the genuineness and veracity of Apollo's
greatest oracle : a belief which not even cases of
corruption like that recorded in Herodotus,[3] or the
frequent ambiguity [4] and obscurity of its responses

[1] Arist. Rhet. 1398 b.

[2] Vid. Jupp. Trag. vi.; Bis Acc. i. We may compare
the sarcastic account which Oenomaus, a Cynic of Hadrian's
time, gives of his visit to the oracle of Apollo at Colophon.
Disgusted as the philosopher was with the first two responses,
the climax came when, to his question as to where he had better
turn to after leaving Colophon, the god bade him " hurl stones
from a long-whirling sling and knock over untold green-feed-
ing ganders," ἐκ τανυστρόφοιο λᾶας σφενδόνης ἱεὶς ἀνὴρ | χῆνας
ἐναρίζειν βολαῖσιν, ἀσπέτους, ποιηβόρους. " Who, pray," the indignant philosopher exclaims, " will explain to me the meaning
of those untold green-feeding ganders ? " (Vid. Euseb. Pr.
Ev. v. 23.)

[3] vi. 66, where Cleomenes bribed the Pythia to give sentence
against Demaratus. Cf. Paus. iii. 4. 3–4 ; Hdt. v. 63 ; Thuc.
v. 16.

[4] Cf. Aesch. P.V. 661–2, . . . αἰολοστόμους | χρησμοὺς ἀσήμους
δυσκρίτως τ' εἰρημένους. The most famous instance of ambiguity
is the oracle given to Croesus : Κροῖσος Ἅλυν διαβὰς μεγάλην ἀρχὴν
καταλύσει, Arist. Rhet. 1407 a. Euseb. Pr. Ev. v. xx. gives

66

The Influence of the Delphic Oracle

(as a result of which more than one was lured to his doom), seem in any way seriously to have undermined.

Such was the belief of the ancients. What are *we* to hold in regard to the genuineness of the Oracle and its responses ? Owing to the relations between the " prophet " and the Pythia [1] there was always the possibility of fraud. What was to prevent the " prophet " from interpreting as he pleased the Pythia's wild, incoherent cries ? Might not the responses (in the words of Jocasta in the *Oedipus Tyrannus*)[2] be " not from Phoebus but from his attendants " ? Yet, that such fraud was the constant practice of the priesthood is not at all probable : how could the Oracle thus maintain its credit so long ? Certainly there seems to

---

it in the same form. Cf. Hdt. i. 53 (who paraphrases it) ; Cic. De Div. ii. 115, "Croesus Halyn penetrans magnam pervertet opum vim." With it we may compare the oracle said to have been given to Pyrrhus, when meditating war upon the Romans : " aio te, Aeacida, Romanos vincere posse." Cic. De Div. ii. 56, § 115, attributes this to Apollo, but Dio Cass. Fr. 40. 6 attributes it to Dodona. Cf. also the three cases quoted by Paus. viii. 11, 10–12, where ambiguity wrought harm owing to wrong interpretation. This ambiguity and obscurity of his oracles earned for Apollo the epithet Λοξίας (from λοξός = *obliquus*). But Plutarch, De Garrul. xvii., says that this ambiguity was designed by the god to make men study logic, ' as being indispensable for all who want to understand him aright." From Eur. Andr. 1103, it would appear that there were professional interpreters of oracles (μάντεις Πυθικοί).

[1] Vid. supr. p. 55 and App. B.

[2] Vid. ll. 711–2, οὐκ ἐρῶ | Φοίβου γ᾽ ἀπ᾽ αὐτοῦ, τῶν δ᾽ ὑπηρετῶν ἄπο.

The Delphic Oracle

have been no conscious fraud at least on the part of the priestess : her frenzy was very real ; for we are told by Plutarch [1] that on one occasion she died as a result of the violent agitation caused by the prophetic *furor*.

Was the Pythia's mind exalted under inspiration to a superhuman knowledge ? Here we must bear in mind certain important facts. In the first place, the Pythia was a very ordinary personage who had " gained nothing from art or training or help of any sort." [2] Secondly, she seems not to have known beforehand the nature of the questions submitted to her. [3] And yet what extraordinary responses is she not said to have given on certain occasions ! [4] But of course we must bear in mind

[1] De Def. Orac. li. Here Plut. says that the catastrophe was due to the fact that the priestess ascended the tripod against her will and was possessed by an " incoherent and evil inspiration " (ἀλάλου καὶ κακοῦ πνεύματος οὖσα πλήρής). Cf. the description of the Pythian frenzy in Lucan, Phars. v. 161 ff. As has been already pointed out, however, we cannot be sure how far it is a statement of fact.

[2] Plut. De Pyth. Orac. xxii.

[3] Cf. Plut. (De Garrul. xx.), who says that " the Pythia was accustomed to give certain responses off-hand even before the question was asked " (ἡ μὲν γὰρ Πυθία καὶ πρὸ ἐρωτήσεως αὐθωρὶ χρησμοὺς εἴωθέ τινας ἐκφέρειν. ὁ γὰρ θεὸς, ᾧ λατρεύει καὶ κωφοῦ συνίησι, καὶ οὐ λαλέοντος ἀκούει). Schol. Arist. Plut. 39, says that questions had to be submitted in writing (ἐγγράφῳ ἀνακοινώσει). These were taken charge of most probably by the " prophet " and priests, who transcribed the response generally in (hexameter) verse. Vid. App. B, p. 189, n. 3.

[4] We have many instances of remarkable Delphic prophecies. Paus. (ix. 14. 3) cites the response which predicted the defeat

The Influence of the Delphic Oracle

the possibility that many of those responses, which are attributed to the Delphic Oracle, may not be authentic, or are mere *post-eventum* prophecies. The pseudo-oracular form is one that has been practised in all ages with considerable success,[1] and there is always a tendency to attribute oracles generally to one well-known source.

Yet there is at least one famous oracle, the authenticity of which seems certain enough—the famous test-oracle of Croesus.[2] The story, though thrice familiar, may be repeated. Croesus, king of Lydia, wished to make war on Cyrus, but feared to do so without the express sanction of heaven. This was to be learned, of course, through the oracles. But it was first necessary to test the veracity of these. Accordingly, he despatched

of the Lacedaemonians at Leuctra: Λεῦκτρά τέ μοι σκιόεντα μέλει καὶ Ἀλήσιον οὖδας, κ.τ.λ. The same author (viii. 11. 10) says that the Oracle predicted the death of Epaminondas. Ep. was told to beware of Πέλαγος. He thought that the *sea* was meant, whereas the god forewarned him against the *wood* Πέλαγος in Arcadia. According to Paus. (viii. 7. 4) the Oracle predicted the death of Philip of Macedon. (Cf. Diod. xvi. 91.) According to Diod. (xvii. 10. 3) the Oracle predicted the destruction of Thebes by Alexander the Great. Suetonius (Nero, 38) tells us that Nero was warned by Pythian Apollo " to beware of 73." He thought he would reign to that age, whereas the Oracle referred to the age of his successor, Galba.

[1] Nor is it unknown in modern times; prophecy regarding the issue of the present World-War has been as rife as it was in the days of Thucydides regarding the Peloponnesian struggle. (Cf. Thuc. ii. 21.)

[2] Hdt. i. 46–8. Cf. Euseb. Pr. Ev. v. 20–1.

69

The Delphic Oracle

envoys to six of the best-known oracles then existing: those of Delphi, Dodona, Branchidae, Zeus Ammon, Trophonius and Amphiaraus. On the hundredth day from their departure, the envoys were to ask these several oracles what was Croesus doing at home in Sardis *at the particular moment.* He had carefully kept the secret to himself, and had chosen an action which was beyond all possible conjecture.

Four oracles failed; Amphiaraus was nearly right. Delphi alone succeeded perfectly. For, no sooner had the envoys put their question than the Pythia answered with exact truth, that Croesus was engaged in boiling " the hard-shelled tortoise " and the flesh of a lamb, " with brass above and brass beneath." [1] The messengers returned with the response to Sardis, and Croesus, delighted beyond measure, despatched the envoys once more to Delphi with magnificent gifts, which were still in the days of Herodotus the glory of the sanctuary.[2] They now asked the practical question about the advisability of Croesus' going to war, and received the famous response that " Croesus by crossing the Halys would destroy a mighty kingdom," [3] the

[1] Hdt. i. 47 :

> ὀδμή μ' ἐς φρένας ἦλθε κραταιρίνοιο χελώνης
> ἑψομένης ἐν χαλκῷ ἅμ' ἀρνείοισι κρέεσσι,
> ᾗ χαλκὸς μὲν ὑπέστρωται, χαλκὸν δ' ἐπίεσται.

[2] Hdt. i. 50–1.

[3] Vid. p. 66, n. 4 for the exact form of the oracle; Hdt. i. 53 merely paraphrases it.

The Influence of the Delphic Oracle

ambiguity of which, unseen by Croesus in his pride, lured him to his doom.[1]

Regarding the latter response, we cannot with any degree of probability maintain that the Pythia had any foreknowledge of the result of the enterprise which Croesus was about to undertake. Indeed, the narrative itself rather proves the contrary. Surely we cannot maintain that the god was deliberately luring by an ambiguous oracle his most devoted worshipper to destruction? The response is rather to be taken as a good example of the manner in which the god could shelter his ignorance behind a studied ambiguity. Yet of two facts we are certain: that Croesus did send " glorious gifts " to Delphi, and did go to war with Cyrus, losing his own " mighty kingdom." [2] Is it not reasonable enough, then, to maintain that the remainder of the story as to the Pythia's knowledge of the secret action of Croesus is genuine? And *if* it is genuine, whence the Pythia's knowledge? She could not have gained it by any purely physical means. Those were not the days of wireless telegraphy or wireless telephony. How, then, must we explain it? It is impossible to say with any degree of certainty. Perhaps it is to be explained by the laws of telepathy, for, especially under abnormal psychic conditions, persons have

[1] For Croesus' complaint against Apollo, as deceiving his benefactors, and the god's reply vid. Hdt. i. 90–1.
[2] Ibid. i. 75 ff.

The Delphic Oracle

shown themselves endowed with a knowledge truly marvellous.[1] These abnormal psychic conditions, in the case of the Pythia, would probably be induced to a certain extent by the course of mantic preparation which she had to perform.[2] The fasting, the drinking from the sacred spring, the chewing of the laurel leaves—these, combined above all with a *strong belief in the reality of the inspiration,* might in a guileless, uneducated soul—especially a woman—produce such an abnormal psychic state, which could induce even the physical phenomena of trance and agitation,[3] such as were associated with the Delphi priestess.

But would this be a sufficient explanation of *all* the facts associated with the Delphic inspiration? It seems doubtful. Pernaps, after all, there is something in the explanation given by Plutarch [4]— that the Pythia's inspiration was due to the influence of "demons," i.e. spirits. His theory reminds us

[1] Vid. an excellent chapter in Hudson's " Psychic Phenomena " (chap. xix.), also Maher, " Psychology," p. 597.

[2] Vid. supr. pp. 53–4 ; cf. the mantic ritual in vogue at Argos, where the priestess of the temple of Apollo had to drink the blood of a lamb, sacrificed by night, thus becoming " possessed of the god " (κάτοχος ἐκ τοῦ θεοῦ), Paus. ii. 24. 1; cf. also the ritual of drinking bull's blood at the prophetic shrine of Ge at Aegaera (near Aegae in Achaea), Paus. vii. 25. 13. This reminds us of a mantic method in vogue in ancient Ireland, where the oracle was given in a dream to a person after eating the flesh of a white bull ; vid. Joyce's "Social Hist. of Iréland," vol. i. p. 245.

[3] Vid. Hudson, l. c.

[4] De Def. Orac. xxxviii. xlviii. li. ; vid. supr. p. 58.

The Influence of the Delphic Oracle

of an incident in "Acts of Apostles." [1]   Here there is
a remarkable instance of a girl " having a pythonical
(i.e. a divining) spirit, who brought to her masters
much gain by divining." She, following St. Paul
and his disciples for many days, kept crying out,
" these men are the servants of the Most High God,
who preach unto you the way of salvation. But
(the narrative continues) Paul, being grieved,
turned and said to the spirit : I command thee in
the name of Jesus Christ to go out from her. And
he went out the same hour." Perhaps it was similar
with the Pythia ; perhaps she, too, had a " divining
spirit," who worked in the interests of her masters,
the Delphic priests. This possible parallelism between the Scriptural narrative and the history of
the Delphic priestess has not, to my knowledge,
been shown.[2]   Certainly the hypothesis that the
Delphic inspiration was due to demon or spirit
influence, would seem amply to account for the
phenomena of the Delphic inspiration—aye, even
in the case of the famous instance recorded by
Plutarch, where the Pythia died as the result of
the prophetic frenzy. This would simply be a case
of violent *possession*, of which Scripture affords us
so many instances. Furthermore, the theory is
borne out by the statements of Plutarch regarding

[1] xvi. 16–8.

[2] Since writing this, however, I find that my hypothesis of
explaining the phenomena of the Pythian inspiration as being
due to *possession* has, in a general way, been anticipated by
F. W. H. Myers, in his " Essay on Greek Oracles," p. 16.

the origin of the Delphic inspiration,[1] and more explicitly still by those of Porphyry, who had first-hand information on the subject. For, according to Eusebius, " he seems to have associated most of all contemporary philosophers with spirits and those whom he calls gods." [2] Porphyry maintains that the source of mantic inspiration was spirits, and gives elaborate rules to be observed for proper spirit intercourse.[3] Yet an hypothesis it remains. It would be desirable of course if we could explain the phenomena of Delphi on purely natural grounds, for it has been well said that " the man who carries his story into the invisible world passes out of the range of criticism." But a purely natural explanation of *all* the facts connected with Delphi does not, I think, seem possible.

I have now dwelt at considerable length on the chief " intrinsic " cause of the influence of the Delphic Oracle—the possession of an enthusiastic μαντική—and the various questions to which it gives rise. My reason for doing so is the surpassing interest of this aspect of the subject, so fascinating for its very obscurity.

There is another " intrinsic " cause, to which I should wish to refer : the skill and vigour of the Oracle's internal administration. There is no necessity to see in all the acts of the Oracle the workings of inspiration : much of its activity, we may feel

---

[1] Vid. supr. p. 58.   [2] Pr. Ev. iv. 6.
[3] Vid. Euseb. Pr. Ev. iv. 1, 5, v. 8, 9, 12, vi. 5.

The Influence of the Delphic Oracle

sure, had its origin with the Apolline priests. These, no doubt, were possessed of a remarkable degree of practical wisdom—the heritage of long ages—which manifested itself in various ways. To this, perhaps, we may attribute their attitude in all religious matters, which, as we shall see, was one of generous tolerance.[1] At any rate, whatever was their motive, this attitude towards the various cults won for Delphi the loyalty of whole communities, which a more repressive policy would probably have alienated. So, too, in the case of the Dionysiac worship,[2] which they so vigorously fostered, it is possible that they were influenced by prudential considerations : they perhaps thought it better to foster and encourage what they dare not interfere with.

Again, the Delphic priests showed themselves ready to keep pace with the growth of general culture and philosophic thought.[3] Towards philosophers, poets and artists generally they showed a spirit of sympathy and appreciation, thus securing the adherence of men who were a power in the ancient world, and whose friendship was worth the fostering. Pythagoras [4] was a close friend of the

[1] Vid. infr. iv. pp. 115–16.   [2] Ibid. and supr. pp. 21–2.
[3] Vid. infr. pp. 145–6.
[4] He was supposed to have been inspired by Apollo and was known at Croton as the " Hyperborean Apollo." Vid. Ael. Var. Hist. ii. 26 ; cf. Diog. Laert. viii. 9. 11.   He was considered the disciple of the Pythia Themistoclea. Vid. Diog. Laert. viii. 19. 21, . . . τὰ δόγματα λαβεῖν αὐτὸν (i.e. Πυθαγόραν) παρὰ τῆς ἐν Δελφοῖς Θεμιστοκλείας.

The Delphic Oracle

Oracle. Socrates was declared by it the wisest of men [1]—certainly a momentous utterance. Plato's esteem for the Oracle was doubtless reciprocated. Aristotle was honoured with a decree of the Delphians for compiling a history of the prize-winners at the Pythian games (Πυθιονῖκαι).[2] Plutarch held the priestly dignity at Delphi and passed his old age there.[3] There, too, celebrated men like Apollonius of Tyana [4] and Dio of Prusa [5] betook themselves and sojourned.

But Apollo was the god not only of philosophers but also of poets. " He drove not from Delphi," says Plutarch, " the honoured Muse from the tripod, but invited her. Nay, rather he aroused the poetic temperaments and inspired himself poetic phantasies." [6] The Pythia bade the Delphians give to Pindar an equal share in all the first-fruits they

---

[1] Vid. infr. p. 145.

[2] An inscription found by the French excavators in the sanctuary of the temple of Delphi gives a decree of the Delphians granting the privilege of " proxenia " to Aristotle and Callisthenes, his nephew, for compiling a history of the Πυθιονῖκαι. That it is the philosopher is proved (1) by the style of writing which dates from that period, (2) by the mention of Callisthenes, (3) by the fact that Diogenes Laertius, Hesychius, Plutarch, etc., attribute such a work to Aristotle. (Vid. Diog. Laert. v. 12, and cf. B.C.H. xx. p. 98.)

[3] Vid. supr. p. 63.

[4] Vid. Philostr. Apollon. of Tyana, iv. 24, vi. 10. Cf. B.C.H. xx. p. 716 for an inscr. ΑΠΟΛΛΩΝΙΟΝ ΟΙ ΜΑΘΗΤΑΙ, which is, perhaps, a monument of his passage.

[5] Vid. supr. p. 64.

[6] De Pyth. Orac. xxiv.

The Influence of the Delphic Oracle

offered to Apollo [1]—a privilege which the poet's posterity enjoyed long years after his death. Day by day the sacrificing priest would bid the poet " come to the supper of the god." [2] At Delphi, too, was the chair upon which Pindar sat when he visited the place and recited his poems.[3] Aristonous of Corinth was honoured with a decree by the Delphians for his Paean to Apollo,[4] and the like honour was conferred upon the author of the Delphic Paean to Dionysus, Philodamus of Scarphia.[5] Cleochares, son of Bion of Athens, author of a Hymn to Apollo, was honoured with public praise and a garland.[6] In the Treasury of the Sicyonians was preserved a " golden book " dedicated by the Erythraean poetess, Aristomache, who had won the prize for poetry at the Isthmian games.[7]

Artists generally were not neglected. At Delphi

---

[1] Vid. Paus. ix. 23. 2, εὐδοκιμοῦντα δὲ αὐτὸν ἤδη ἀνὰ πᾶσαν τὴν Ἑλλάδα ἐς πλέον δόξης ἦρεν ἡ Πυθία ἀνειποῦσα Δελφοῖς, ὁπόσων ἀπήρχοντο τῷ Ἀπόλλωνι, μοῖραν καὶ Πινδάρῳ τὴν ἴσην ἀπάντων νέμειν.

[2] Vid. Eustath. Vita Pind. : Ἀπόλλων γοῦν οὕτω φασὶν αὐτὸν ἐφίλει, ὡς καὶ μερίδα λαμβάνειν ἐκ τῶν θυομένων ἐκείνῳ καὶ τὸν ἱερέα δὲ βοᾶν ἐν ταῖς θυσίαις " Πίνδαρος ἐπὶ τὸ δεῖπνον τῷ θεῷ," ἢ καὶ ἄλλως " Πίνδαρος ἴτω ἐπὶ τὸ δεῖπνον τοῦ θεοῦ." . That the poet's posterity continued to enjoy this privilege is clear from Plut. De Sera Num· Vind. xiii.: ἀναμνήσθητι δὲ τῶν ἔναγχος τῶν θεοξενίων καὶ τῆς καλῆς ἐκείνης μερίδος, ἣν ἀφαιροῦντες τοὺς Πινδάρου κηρύττουσι λαμβάνειν ἀπογόνους.

[3] Vid. Paus. x. 24. 5.   [4] Vid. B.C.H. xvii. p. 561.

[5] Vid. B.C.H. xix. p. 393.   [6] Vid. B.C.H. xvii. p. 569.

[7] Vid. Frazer, " Comm. Paus." x. 11. 1, quoting from Polemo. For such dedication cf. also the dedication of Satyrus, son of Eumenes, a Samian ; vid. B.C.H. xvii. p. 85.

The Delphic Oracle

were to be found works by the greatest masters of antiquity—monuments reared to the fame of their authors. There was the famous painting of Polygnotus in the Lesche of the Cnidians, the descent of Odysseus into Hades [1]; there, too, was the masterpiece in bronze, " Alexander's chase," by Lysippus [2]; there, also, was the work of the great Praxiteles.[3] Even lesser artists—actors,[4] musicians,[5] public reciters [6]—were honoured at Delphi. Athletes [7] of all kinds received even extravagant honours, some of them being actually raised to the

[1] Vid. Paus. x. 23-31, with Frazer's " Comm." Cf. F. W. H. Myers, " Essays," p. 50 ff.

[2] Plin. xxxiv. The dedication of this celebrated work was discovered by the French, but no trace of the figures could be found. Vid. *B.C.H.* xxi. p. 599.

[3] Cf. the golden statue of Phryne, Plut. De Pyth. Orac. xiv. ; Paus. x. 15. 1.

[4] Cf. " Artists of Dionysus " ($\tau\epsilon\chi\nu\hat{\iota}\tau\alpha\iota\ \Delta\iota\sigma\nu\acute{\upsilon}\sigma\sigma\upsilon$), for honours given to whom vid. infr. iv. p. 118.

[5] Vid. *B.C.H.* xviii. pp. 85, 97. Musaeus, a $\chi\sigma\rho\alpha\upsilon\lambda\acute{\eta}s$ from Magnesia on the Menander, and M. Turanio, a $\kappa\iota\theta\alpha\rho\psi\delta\acute{\sigma}s$ (who had been victorious in the Pythian games), were honoured with a decree granting the former the privilege of $\pi\rho\sigma\xi\epsilon\nu\acute{\iota}\alpha$ and a garland, and the latter the usual $\pi\rho\sigma\mu\alpha\nu\tau\epsilon\acute{\iota}\alpha$, $\pi\rho\sigma\delta\iota\kappa\acute{\iota}\alpha$, etc.

[6] Vid. *B.C.H.* xviii. p. 80. The brothers Cleodorus and Thrasybulus, who gave public recitations ($\epsilon\pi\iota\delta\epsilon\acute{\iota}\xi\epsilon\iota s$) from the works of the ancient poets, were honoured with a decree by the Delphians. Similarly we find a decree in honour of a historian (who is probably Zenodotus of Troezen) for having recited at Delphi extracts ($\mathring{\alpha}\kappa\rho\sigma\acute{\alpha}\sigma\epsilon\iota s$) from his history (vid. *B.C.H.* xviii. p. 77).

[7] Vid. *B.C.H.* xviii. p. 70 for a long list of decrees and dedications in honour of athletes, as well as prize-winners at musical contests, of whom Pausanias (x. 9) took but such scant notice.

The Influence of the Delphic Oracle

rank of heroes.[1] Thus did the Delphic Oracle cater for men of every rank, profession, and intellect.

Such, then, or such-like, were the causes which contributed to the remarkable growth and spread of the influence of the Delphic Oracle, causes varied and complex. Yet from this very complexity sprang a force and vitality such as no other oracle of antiquity knew.

[1] Vid. infr. iv. pp. 124–5.

CHAPTER III

POLITICAL INFLUENCE OF THE DELPHIC ORACLE

SECTION A: GENERAL RELATIONS OF THE ORACLE IN POLITICS

THE history of ancient Greece shows a remarkable closeness of relations between politics and religion —a closeness that is somewhat surprising to the modern world, which so often sees separation, or even overt hostility, between Church and State. To the mind of the Greek such hostility of the State towards religion would be a piece of insolent pride and folly, which was sure to call down the nemesis of Heaven. For the success alike of the State and the individual the good-will of the gods was essential: no institution could flourish, no project be successful, for which there was not the divine sanction.[1] But the will of the gods was to be known, and their sanction to be obtained, above all through

---

[1] This is especially true of Sparta, which sought oracles for everything; cf. Cic. De Div. i. 95, " Lacedaemonii de rebus maioribus semper aut Delphis oraculum aut ab Hammone aut a Dodona petebant "; cf. ibid. i. 63. So, too, it was with the Romans, vid. Cic. De Div. i. 2, § 3, " Exactis regibus nihil publice sine auspiciis nec domi nec militiae gerebatur."

Political Influence of the Delphic Oracle

their oracles, and of these none was truer, none more trustworthy, than that of Pythian Apollo.

The practice of consulting oracles in public and private interests dates from the days of Homer.[1] But the political consultation of Delphi seems to date from a comparatively late period. We have only one instance in Homer,[2] where we are told how Agamemnon " o'erstepped the threshold of stone in hallowed Pytho " to consult the Oracle of Phoebus Apollo. In the ninth book of the *Iliad*,[3] however, Achilles speaks of Delphi (under the name of Pytho) as already proverbial for its wealth.[4] He would not barter his life, he says, " for all the treasures that the stone-threshold of the Archer, Phoebus, containeth in rocky Pytho." This wealth we may assume to have accumulated in no other

[1] Od. xvi. 403–5, xiv. 327–30. It must be noted, however, that these two cases refer to oracles of Zeus, the second expressly mentioning Dodona " of the high leafy oak-tree." There is no mention of political consultation in the Iliad, which is probably much older than the Odyssey; vid. Jebb, "Gr. Lit." p. 37.

[2] Od. viii. 79–81. The passage, however, seems comparatively late; cf. Farnell, op. cit. p. 194.

[3] Vid. ll. 404–5:

> οὐδ᾽ ὅσα λάϊνος οὐδὸς Ἀφήτορος ἔντος ἐέργει
> Φοίβου Ἀπόλλωνος, Πυθοῖ ἔνι πετρηέσσῃ.

[4] For the wealth of Delphi cf. Soph. O.T. 151–2, τῆς πολυχρύσου Πυθῶνος; Eur. Andr. 1093, θεοῦ | χρυσοῦ γέμοντα γύαλα, θησαυροὺς βροτῶν; Pind. P.. vi. 8–9. The temple treasury was a sort of bank in which gold and silver could be deposited till required for use. Cf. Thuc. i. 121 ; Eur. Ion, 54.

The Delphic Oracle

way than in later times, namely, from the offerings of consultants (ἀναθήματα),[1] seeking aid and light in matters of public and private import. The book, however, was probably not part of the original *Iliad* : if it dated from the same period as the rest of the *Iliad*, we should surely expect to see more references to the Oracle throughout the poem.[2]

Such habitual consultation of an oracle for political purposes naturally endowed the priesthood in ancient times with extraordinary power—a power

---

[1] For examples of such ἀναθήματα vid. (α) Hdt. i. 25 : the famous bowl of Alyattes, only the stand of which remained in Pausanias's time (x. 16. 1–2); (β) id. ii. 135, and Paus. x. 14. 7 : the altar of the Chians, the remains of which have been discovered by the French excavators (vid. Homolle in *B.C.H.* xvii. p. 614, and xviii. p. 179 ff.) in the exact position described by Hdt. ; the cornice of the temple bears the inscr. ΧΙΟΙ ΑΠΟΛΛΩΝΙ ΤΟΝ ΒΩΜΟΝ ; (γ) Hdt. i. 50–1 : the golden lion, bowls, etc., offered by Croesus (because Delphi alone had stood the famous test) ; (δ) id. i. 14, the golden bowls presented by Gyges ; (ε) Paus. x. 13. 9 : the famous tripod of gold dedicated by the Greeks for the victory at Plataea ; the base, which supported it, is believed to have been discovered by the French ; (ζ) Diod. xi. 26. 7 : the golden tripod of Gelon (the work of Bion, son of Diodorus of Miletus), ruler of Syracuse, which was dedicated by him in commemoration of the victory over the Carthaginians at Himera, 480 B.C. Apparently there were four tripods in all : one for G. himself, and one for each of his three brothers—though Diod. mentions only one—for the French excavators found four sockets together, each of which apparently held a tripod. On one was an inscr. giving clearly Gelon's name (*B.C.H.* xxi. p. 588). Vid. infr. p. 93.

[2] Cf. Grote, " Hist. Gr." ii. p. 285 ; Hom. Il., Leaf and Bayfield, Introd. xxi.

Political Influence of the Delphic Oracle

which they sometimes abused. Thus Plutarch [1] tells us that the Aenianes, when they lived in the Cirrhaean plain, were ordered by an oracle— probably the Delphian—to stone their king. This, however, would probably have been, not so much a sacerdotal oppression of a particular dynasty, as an instance of piacular human sacrifice, which, as we shall see, was not unfrequently prescribed by Delphi. So, too, according to Diodorus,[2] the Aethiopian king was accustomed to commit suicide at the bidding of the priests of Meroe. The tradition remained unbroken till the time of the Ptolemies, when a king massacred the priests and destroyed the shrine.

No serious abuse of power, however, can be laid to the charge of the Delphic priesthood. Notwithstanding their exceptional opportunities for self-aggrandisement, the priests of Apollo do not seem to have grasped at unlawful gain : they appear on the whole to have faithfully observed the behests of the god in the Homeric Hymn, and to have contented themselves with the offerings " which the renowned tribes of men should bring." [3] With these indeed they were passing rich, as is clearly shown by the many refer-

[1] Quaest. Gr. 13 : ἐν δὲ τῇ Κίρρῃ καταλεύσαντες Οἴνοπλον τὸν βασιλέα, τοῦ θεοῦ προστάξαντος, κ.τ.λ. ; cf. Farnell, op. cit. iv. p. 195.

[2] iv. p. 195.

[3] Hom. Hymn. Ap. 537 : ὅσσα ἐμοὶ κἀγάγωσι περικλυτὰ φῦλ' ἀνθρώπων.

The Delphic Oracle

ences to the " gold-filled hollows of the god " and
" Pytho rich in gold." [1] As long as they could
maintain intact the prestige of the Oracle, affluence
was secured to them. The insignificance, too, of
the Delphic state, from whose oldest families the
priesthood was drawn,[2] saved the shrine from form-
ing dangerous schemes for the increase of temporal
power. In its political dealings with states as
well as with individuals the Oracle held the balance
of justice evenly enough [3]—sometimes even in
difficult circumstances. We see from Herodotus [4]
how the Oracle dissuaded the Lacedaemonians from
attacking Arcadia. It must be admitted, however,
that it urged them on to the attack of the Tegeans.
At times, nevertheless, we notice a certain partiality
in the utterances of the Oracle, above all, towards
Sparta.[5] It is not surprising, however, that the
Oracle should thus have leanings towards Sparta,
owing to the constant close relations existing between them.[6] Sometimes it shows a partiality even

[1] Vid. supr. pp. 81–2.

[2] Cf. Δελφῶν ἀριστῆς, Eur. Ion, 416, also κοίρανοι Πυθικοί and
Δελφῶν ἄνακτες (ibid. 1219, 1222). Vid. App. B.

[3] Instances of corruption like that mentioned in Hdt. vi. 66
do not affect the general truth of the statement.

[4] i. 66, cf. Paus. viii. 1. 6 ; Bury, " Hist. Gr." p. 202.

[5] Cf. Thuc. i. 118, where the Oracle predicts victory for
Sparta and declares its resolution to assist the Lacedaemonians,
whether asked or not ; cf. also Thuc. ii. 54.

[6] For instances of close relations between Sparta and Delphi
vid. Plat. Legg. 624 A ; Xen. Rep. Laced. viii. 5 ; Plut.
De Pyth. Orac. xix. (Delphic origin of Lycurgan constitu-

84

Political Influence of the Delphic Oracle

towards the Athenians, particularly the powerful family of the Alcmaeonidae. These had assiduously cultivated the friendship of the Delphic priests: they had built on a magnificent scale the temple of Apollo which had been burned down in 548 B.C.[1] This fact probably accounts for the action of the Oracle in urging the Lacedaemonians to expel the Pisistratidae from Athens,[2] and thus pave the way for the return of the long-exiled Alcmaeonidae.[3]

Delphi, then, was dependent for its subsistence upon the charity of Apollo's worshippers.[4] Yet

tion; for Cretan origin, however, vid. Hdt. i. 65); Hdt. v. 63–5 (expulsion of the Pisistratidae from Athens by Sparta at the instance of the Oracle); Thuc. i. 112 (restoration by the Lacedaemonians of the temple of Delphi to the Delphians, which had been seized by the Phocians). Cf. also the legend of the colonization of Peloponnesus at the bidding of the Oracle This is probably true : it would explain the closeness of relations between the Spartans and the Delphic Oracle. Yet we shall find the Oracle rebuking Spartan pride and avarice (vid. infr. p. 146).

[1] Vid. Hdt. v. 62. The Amphictyons contracted with the Alcmaeonidae for the rebuilding of the temple (vid. Hdt. ii. 180). Some traces of the temple of the Alcmaeonidae were found by the French excavators, sufficient to give a fairly adequate idea of the architecture. Vid. *B.C.H.* xx. p. 646.

[2] For the expulsion of the Pisistratidae vid. Hdt. v. 63–5, and cf. Bury, " Hist. Gr." p. 205 ff. For the suspicion that the Alcmaeonidae had bribed the Pythia to propose constantly to the Spartans to liberate Athens vid. Hdt. v. 63.

[3] For the story of the conspiracy of Cylon, 632 B.C., and the expulsion of the Alcmaeonidae vid. Hdt. v. 71–2 ; Thuc. i. 126 ; cf. Bury, " Hist. Gr." pp. 178–9.

[4] Cf. Hom. Hymn. Ap. 528 ff. and infr. p. 90.

The Delphic Oracle

this very dependence, while it saved the Apolline priests from indulging in dangerous, ambitious schemes, seems to have been the source of that weak-kneed and vacillating policy which the Oracle displayed even in the darkest hour of Greece. The thought that the source of all their subsistence lay within the precincts of the god inspired the Delphic priests with a spirit of over-cautiousness and timidity, which made them tremble at the onset of the foe. To them the advancing Xerxes with his innumerable host seemed irresistible. They were probably among those who saw in the great king not a man but a god.[1] In their nervous timidity they pictured to themselves the ruined shrines,[2] the rifled treasures, all Greece prostrate at the feet of the barbarian with his strange gods and barbaric ways. And so when the two envoys of the Athenians came to consult the god, no sooner had they entered the oracular precinct than the Pythia, Aristonice,

[1] Cf. Hdt. vii. 203. At an earlier period we find the god counselling the Cnidians to surrender to the Persian general, Harpagus (Hdt. i. 174, cf. Euseb. Pr. Ev. v. 26. 3).

[2] They had warning, it is true, in the treatment meted out to the shrine of Apollo of Branchidae (Hdt. vi. 19), which the Persians had pillaged and burned after the fall of Miletus, 494 B.C. That their fears were not wholly groundless was proved by the fact that Xerxes, on his march to Athens, did actually send a detachment to plunder the Delphic shrine. The attack, however, according to the story in Herodotus (viii. 36–9), was miraculously repulsed. For lightnings from heaven smote the barbarians as they approached, and two crags torn from Parnassus spread havoc amongst them, whilst two superhuman warriors aided the Delphians in the slaughter of the fugitives.

exclaimed : " O wretched men, why sit ye here ?
Fly to the ends of the earth, leaving your homes
and the topmost heights of your wheel-shaped city.
For, neither does the head remain firm, nor the
body, nor the extremities of the feet, nor yet the
hands, nor is aught of the middle left—all is in evil
plight. For fire and fierce Ares, driving the Syrian
car, destroys it, and he will lay low many other
fenced cities, and not yours alone. Many temples
of the gods he will deliver to devouring fire, which
now stand dripping with sweat, quaking with fear.
And upon their roof-tops black blood is shed, har-
binger of inevitable woe. Depart ye from my
sanctuary with your souls steeped in sorrow." [1]
Such was the wail of despair which broke from the
shrine of Apollo in the blackest hour of Hellas !
Such the consolation that the Panhellenic sanctuary

[1] Hdt. vii. 140:

> Ὦ μέλεοι, τί κάθησθε; λιπὼν φεῦγ' ἔσχατα γαίης
> δώματα καὶ πόλιος τροχοειδέος ἄκρα κάρηνα.
> οὔτε γὰρ ἡ κεφαλὴ μένει ἔμπεδον, οὔτε τὸ σῶμα,
> οὔτε πόδες νέατοι, οὔτ' ὦν χέρες, οὔτε τι μέσσης, κ.τ.λ.

Cf. Euseb. Pr. Ev. v. 24. Some (cf. L. and S. s.v. ἐπικίδνημι)
trans. the closing words of the Oracle, κακοῖς δ' ἐπικίδνατε θυμόν, as
" bear a brave heart amid woes," " spread a brave spirit over
your ills." But this rendering seems to me utterly against the
context. The word οἱ (l. 9 of the oracle) may refer to the
temples (cf. altar of Neptune sweating, Liv. xxviii. 11), or to
the gods themselves (i.e. their images), which sometimes ran
sweat or blood (cf. Diod. xvii. 10, 5 ; Liv. xxii. 1 ; Cic. De
Div. i. 34, § 74, " Herculisque simulacrum multo sudore mana-
vit," and Milton, " And the chill marble seems to sweat,"
" Hymn on the Nativity," 195).

87

The Delphic Oracle

could offer, when, if ever, counsels of help and hope were needed ! Little wonder is it that the envoys, when they heard it, were filled with the deepest dejection and dare not bring this answer to Athens. Fortunately, however, all at Delphi did not share in the faint-heartedness of the Oracle. There was a certain influential Delphian, named Timon, who advised them to take supplicatory branches—he knew that the god's decision was not immutable—and in the guise of suppliants approach the Oracle a second time. This they did. " O King, vouchsafe," they said, " some better response regarding our country, reverencing these suppliant boughs wherewith we are come to thee; else we depart not from thy shrine but remain here till death." And lo ! the god was changed ! This time he held out some hope ! The Pythia replied : " Athene, entreating with her many prayers and prudent counsel, cannot propitiate Olympian Zeus. But to thee again I will address this word, making it like unto adamant. For, when all is taken that the boundary of Cecrops encloses and the recesses of sacred Cithaeron, wide-seeing Zeus gives to the Triton-born a wooden wall to be alone impregnable, which shall preserve thee and thy children. Nor do thou quietly await the cavalry and infantry that in a mighty host are advancing from the mainland, but turn thy back and withdraw. Thou shalt yet live to fight another day. O Salamis divine, thou shalt cause the sons of women to perish when the corn is scattered

Political Influence of the Delphic Oracle

or gathered." [1] Such was the Pythia's second response to the distressed envoys, which, ambiguous and obscure though it was, brought them some consolation. This second response, just as the first, probably counselled flight—so the official interpreters explained it—but the genius of Themistocles came to the rescue of the Oracle and saved its credit. For, he interpreted " the wooden walls " to refer to the ships, and forthwith counselled the Athenians to abandon their city and make preparations for a sea fight.[2] The great victory at " divine Salamis," due primarily to the Athenians,[3] proved the saving of Hellas, and the Greeks in the joy of their deliverance from the impending calamity offered first-fruits to the Delphic god,[4] ascribing

[1] Hdt. vii. 141 :

> οὐ δύναται Παλλὰς Δί' 'Ολύμπιον ἐξιλάσασθαι,
> λισσομένη πολλοῖσι λόγοις καὶ μήτιδι πυκνῇ.
> σοὶ δὲ τόδ' αὖτις ἔπος ἐρέω, ἀδάμαντι πελάσσας·
> τῶν ἄλλων γὰρ ἁλισκομένων, ὅσα Κέκροπος οὖρος
> ἐντὸς ἔχει κευθμών τε Κιθαιρῶνος ζαθέοιο, κ.τ.λ.

Both these responses are undoubtedly genuine, for who after the glorious victory at Salamis would have been the author of such gloomy utterances ? Furthermore, we find an adaptation of the first in Aesch. Pers. 81 ff. Some think that the last two lines of the second response, 'Ω θείη Σαλαμίς, ἀπολεῖς δὲ σὺ τέκνα γυναικῶν, κ.τ.λ., are a later addition, but there is nothing in the context to prove that they are not genuine.

[2] Hdt. vii. 143 : παρασκευάζεσθαι ὧν αὐτοὺς ὡς ναυμαχήσοντας συνεβούλευε, ὡς τούτου ἐόντος τοῦ ξυλίνου τείχεος.

[3] Ibid. vii. 139 : νῦν δὲ 'Αθηναίους ἄν τις λέγων σωτῆρας γενέσθαι τῆς 'Ελλάδος, οὐκ ἂν ἁμαρτάνοι τὸ ἀληθές.

[4] Ibid. viii. 121 ; according to Hdt. (vii. 178), the Delphians acquired a claim to "everlasting gratitude" (χάριν ἀθάνατον

to him the victory which they owed to one thing only—the genius of Themistocles.

Another result of this dependence of the Apolline priests was that they could have no marked political propaganda. The Delphians, whose rocky soil verily " had not fatness beneath the earth," so that the Cretans summoned over the sea from wooded Cnossus might well exclaim : " this fair land bears not vines, nor is it rich in meadows, wherefrom we might live well and minister unto men " [1]—the Delphians had to be as accommodating as possible in matters political. They had to be all things to all worshippers at the shrine, on whose charity they were dependent.[2] Drawing their clientèle from men of all shades of political opinion, they could not afford to alienate any of their patrons by committing themselves to any marked political programme. And so we find king,

κατέθεντο) " for having communicated to the terrified Greeks the response of the Oracle given to them—that they (the Delphians) should pray to the winds, for these would be great allies of the Greeks." The fate which had befallen the fleet of Mardonius at Athos would naturally suggest to the timid Oracle to make such a request. Apparently, when the danger was all past, the Oracle plucked up sufficient courage to declare the soil of Greece polluted by the presence of the barbarian, and ordered a general purification (Plut. Aristid. xx.).

[1] Hom. Hymn. Ap. 529–30 : οὔτε τρυγηφόρος ἥδε γ' ἐπήρατος, οὔτ' εὐλείμων, | ὥστ' ἀπό τ' εὖ ζώειν καὶ ἄμ' ἀνθρώποισιν ὀπηδεῖν.

[2] Cf. Plut. De Pyth. Orac. xxvi. : ἀλλὰ πόλεις μέγα δυνάμεναι καὶ βασιλεῖς καὶ τύραννοι μέτριον οὐδὲν φρονοῦντες, ἐνετύγχανον τῷ θεῷ περὶ πραγμάτων· οὓς ἀνιᾶν καὶ παροξύνειν ἀπεχθείᾳ πολλὰ τῶν ἀβουλήτων ἀκούοντας οὐκ ἐλυσιτέλει τοῖς περὶ τὸ χρηστήριον.

Political Influence of the Delphic Oracle

oligarch, democrat, all received with open arms, particularly, we may feel sure, " when bringing gifts." The gifts doubtless were welcome, whether the consultant came " on a bootless errand " or not.[1]

Section B : Attitude of the Delphic Oracle towards Tyrants

The Delphic priesthood, however, representing as it did the aristocratic and conservative spirit which held sway in the Dorian states, and which was the reputed author of that " god-built liberty," which Pindar [2] eulogizes, may have felt a genuine dislike for *tyranny*. According to Herodotus [3] the Oracle administered a stern rebuke to the tyrant, Clisthenes of Sicyon. This would seem rather ungrateful, for Clisthenes had championed the cause of Delphi in the First Sacred War (having in 595 B.C. aided the Amphictyons against Cirrha),[4] and had joined in the re-institution of the Pythian festival in 582 B.C.[5] Going to Delphi, he consulted the Oracle as to whether he should expel Adrastus. The Pythia replied that Adrastus was king of the

---

[1] Cf. Hom. Hymn. Merc. 549: ἀλίην ὁδὸν εἶσιν, ἐγὼ δέ κε δῶρα δεχοίμην. For a remarkable instance of rejected gifts, however —the case of Themistocles offering some of the spoils of the Medes after Salamis—vid. Paus. x. 14. 5. It seems strange that the Oracle should have rejected his gifts alone, though it actually enjoined them on the Aeginetans (Hdt. viii. 122).

[2] θεόδματος ἐλευθερία, P. i. 61.

[3] v. 67.

[4] Paus. ii. 9. 6 ; x. 37. 6.   [5] Paus. x. 7. 6.

The Delphic Oracle

Sicyonians, but Clisthenes was their oppressor.[1]
Probably, however, the oracle is a product of a
later day, when Dorian Sparta was all-powerful at
Delphi and blackened the fame of the anti-Dorian
tyrants.[2]

As to the action of the Oracle in getting the
Lacedaemonians to expel the Pisistratidae from
Athens, it does not seem to have been disinterested,
as has been already shown. According to Plutarch,[3]
the Oracle was not favourably disposed towards the
great Sicilian tyrants of the fifth century B.C. He
tells us how, when Dinomenes, the Sicilian, consulted it about his sons, the Oracle replied that all
three should be tyrants. And when Dinomenes
answering said, " To their sorrow, my lord Apollo,"

---

[1] Ἄδρηστον μὲν εἶναι Σικυωνίων βασιλέα, ἐκεῖνον δὲ λευστῆρα. The
word λευστῆρα here is best translated (with Hesych.) as " oppressor," Lat. *lapidator*. Suidas makes it passive, " one worthy
to be stoned " (ὁ καταλευσθῆναι ἄξιος). Some take it to mean
" stone-thrower " : C. was a mere stone-thrower, i.e. not deserving
panoply, much less a sceptre. This last, however, is not a
natural rendering.

[2] Clisthenes was a bitter anti-Dorian, and in derision changed
the names of the Dorian tribes from Hylleis, Dymanes, and
Pamphyli to Hyatae, Choeriatae, and Oneatae (i.e. pigs and asses),
vid. Hdt. v. 68. Hdt. was a hater of tyrants, and his picture
of them is one of almost unrelieved blackness. Cf. his account
of Polycrates (iii. 39–47, 54–6, 120–6), of the Corinthian tyrants
(iii. 48–53, v. 92), of the Ionian tyrants (iv. 136–42).

[3] De Pyth. Orac. xix.: Δεινομένους δὲ τοῦ Σικελιώτου μαντευομένου
περὶ τῶν υἱέων, ἀνεῖλεν ὡς οἱ τρεῖς τυραννήσοιεν. ὑποτυχόντος δὲ τοῦ
Δεινομένους, οἰμωξόμενοί γε, ὦ δέσποτα Ἄπολλον, καὶ τοῦτό σοι (ἔφη)
διδόναι καὶ προσαναιρεῖν.

the Pythia replied, " This, too, do I bestow upon thee, and give by way of addition to the response." All this, however, is probably again but a late invention. Whatever may be said about Dinomenes himself, certainly the relations of his sons with the Oracle seem to have been friendly. We have seen how one of them certainly—and probably all four —presented the god with valuable gifts.[1] So that unless this is a case of the god's accepting gifts, though the giver came " on a bootless errand," we have fairly reliable evidence of the god's reciprocal good-will.

Plutarch also tells us how Procles, tyrant of Epidaurus, had destroyed many people cruelly and unjustly. And when Timarchus had come to him from Athens with money, after receiving him with a show of friendship, he murdered him by the hand

---

[1] **Vid.** p. 82. On one of the sockets on the monumental base found by the French excavators at the summit of the Sacred Way, near the Omphalos and the tripod of Plataea, is an inscription with the dedication quite intact :

> Γέλον ὁ Δεινομένεος
> ἀνέθηκε τἀπόλλονι
> Συρακόσιος . . . . . .
> τὸν τρίποδα καὶ τὲν νίκεν ἐργάσατο
> βίον Διόδορο υἱος Μίλεσιος.

A second inscription, though very mutilated, must be referred to Hiero. Two other sockets of tripods have been found near them. The supposition is that the four sons of Dinomenes (Gelon, Hiero, Thrasybulus and Polyzelus) were represented by four tripods, but those of Gelon and Hiero were the most important and alone bore inscriptions. Vid. *B.C.H.* xxi. p. 588. Diodorus (xi. 26. 7) refers only to one tripod.

The Delphic Oracle

of Cleander of Aegina, and had his body placed in a hamper and cast into the sea. Though these acts were secret, he was afterwards troubled by his guilty conscience and sent his brother Cleotimus to consult the Oracle in private as to the best means of escape and emigration. The god replied that " he granted Procles escape and emigration to where he had bidden his Aeginetan friend to deposit the hamper, or else where the stag sheds his horn." [1] The tyrant, understanding the god to mean that he should either drown or bury himself, waited a little, but was soon driven into exile. But the friends of Timarchus seized him, and having put him to death cast his body into the sea.

Diodorus gives oracular verses ascribed to the Pythian Oracle which speak of " two ways that are very far apart, the one leading to the honoured house of freedom, the other to the house of thraldom to be shunned of mortals." [2] He also gives a speech of the Oracle contrasting the tyranny of Arcesilaus at Cyrene with the milder and freer rule of Battus.[3]

[1] De Pyth. Orac. xix.: ἀνεῖλεν οὖν ὁ θεὸς διδόναι Προκλεῖ φυγὴν καὶ μετάστασιν, ὅπου τὸν φορμὸν ἐκέλευσε καταθέσθαι τὸν Αἰγινήτην ξένον, ἢ ὅπου τὸ κέρας ἀποβάλλει ὁ ἔλαφος.

[2] vii. Fr. 12 :

εἰσιν ὁδοὶ δύο πλεῖστον ἀπ' ἀλλήλων ἀπέχουσαι,
ἢ μὲν ἐλευθερίας εἰς τίμιον οἶκον ἄγουσα,
ἡ δ' ἐπὶ δουλείας φευκτὸν δόμον ἡμερίοισι, κ.τ.λ.

Cf. Euseb. Pr. Ev. v. 28. 7, who also quotes the verses.

[3] viii. Fr. 30.

Political Influence of the Delphic Oracle

Such are the highly edifying stories of the attitude of the Delphic Oracle towards tyrants. Unfortunately, however, we have no means of discovering how far these oracles are genuine, or how far they are mere inventions of a later age. They are of value, however, as showing what kind of political character the Greeks of antiquity associated with Pythian Apollo.

Indeed, occasionally we meet with stories which seem to show that the Oracle did not always maintain this exemplary attitude. We are told in Herodotus[1] how Cypselus, son of Aetion, got a rather favourable response, on the strength of which he attacked and took possession of Corinth, where his thirty years' reign was marked by cruelty and violence. Cypselus afterwards made a return to the Oracle by erecting the Treasury, which, however, was afterwards called that of the Corinthians.[2] For, after the overthrow of the Cypselidae, the Delphians gave permission to the Corinthians to have the dedication changed (though the Eleans refused a like favour at Olympia). Athenaeus[3] also tells us of an oracle from Delphi in behalf of the life of Phalaris, the cruel tyrant

[1] v. 92 ; cf. the oracle which encouraged Cylon to make the attempt upon Athens (Thuc. i. 126): χρωμένῳ δὲ τῷ Κύλωνι ἐν Δελφοῖς ἀνεῖλεν ὁ θεὸς ἐν τοῦ Διὸς τῇ μεγίστῃ ἑορτῇ καταλαβεῖν τὴν Ἀθηναίων ἀκρόπολιν.

[2] Cf. Hdt. i. 14 ; Plut. De Pyth. Orac. xiii.

[3] 602 B. Cf. Euseb. Pr. Ev. v. 35. 2 : Λοξίας καὶ Ζεὺς πατὴρ ἀναβολὴν ἐψηφίσαντο θανάτου Φαλάριδι.

The Delphic Oracle

of Agrigentum. Finally, the name of Periander of Corinth was included at Delphi among the list of the Seven Sages of Greece.[1]

Section C : Pythian Apollo as 'Αρχηγέτης, or Leader of Colonists

In one sphere of its activity, however, the Delphic Oracle merits unqualified praise—the matter of colonization. This, beyond all things else, bears testimony to the sagacity of the Pythian shrine. In the history of Greek colonization we find Pythian Apollo its guide and stimulus throughout. He is the Great Founder ('Αρχηγέτης) [2] under whose guidance the colony is led forth from the mother-city and planted in its new home. " Phoebus ever delights in the founding of cities, and with his own hand lays their foundation." [3] It was the constant custom of all Greek peoples that no colony should

[1] Plut. De E apud Delph. iii. According to Plut. (ibid.), however, both Periander of Corinth and Cleobulus of Lindus " though they had no share in either virtue or wisdom, yet through their power, friends, and interest forcibly took possession of the character and usurped the name of the wise men " (ἔπει δὲ Κλεόβουλος ὁ Λινδίων τύραννος, εἶτα Περίανδρος ὁ Κορίνθιος, οὐδὲν αὐτοῖς ἀρετῆς μετόν, οὐδὲν σοφίας, κ.τ.λ.).

[2] Cf. the epithets Οἰκιστής, Κτίστης. For the epithet 'Αρχηγέτης vid. Pind. P. v. 60: ὁ δ' 'Αρχαγέτας . . . 'Απόλλων; vid. P.W. (s.v. Apollon), 44, for full list of references.

[3] Callim. Hymn. Ap. 56: Φοῖβος γὰρ ἀεὶ πολίεσσι φιληδεῖ | κτιζομένησ', αὐτὸς δὲ θεμείλια Φοῖβος ὑφαίνει. Cf. Lucan, Phars. v. 107, " saepe dedit (sc. Apollo) sedem totas mutantibus urbes."

96

be sent out without the direction and encouragement of the Delphic shrine,[1] and woe to the oekist who started without its sanction and blessing. We may feel sure that Herodotus was but voicing the average sentiment of the fifth-century Greeks in attributing the disasters which befell Dorieus to the fact that he led out a colony "without having consulted the Oracle at Delphi as to what land he should go to to found a colony or having conformed to any of the customary regulations."[2]

How is it that Delphi had such influence in the matter of colonization? The reason was that for Greeks as well as for Romans the founding of a colony was a religious act, like the building of a temple. A new colony was in reality a new sanctuary in which the gods of the mother-city would take up their abode. Now to purify and consecrate the place where the gods would take up their abode naturally came within the domain of religion; but the place where the gods willed their new sanctuary to be erected had first to be pointed out,

[1] Cf. Cic. De Div. i. 1, § 3, " quam vero Graecia coloniam misit in Aeoliam, Ioniam, Asiam, Siciliam, Italiam, sine Pythio aut Dodonaeo aut Hammonis oraculo?" Cf. Plut. De Pyth. Orac. xxvii.

[2] v. 42: οὔτε τῷ ἐν Δελφοῖς χρηστηρίῳ χρησάμενος, ἐς ἥντινα γῆν κτίσων ἴῃ, οὔτε ποιήσας οὐδὲν τῶν νομιζομένων. Cf. ibid. 45 : Δωριέος τὸν θάνατον μαρτύριον μέγιστον ποιεῦνται, ὅτι παρὰ τὰ μεμαντευμένα ποιέων διεφθάρη. Besides consulting the Oracle the oekist (who had to be from the mother-city) must take the holy-fire from the Prytaneum of the mother-city, vid. Thuc. i. 24; "Et. Mag." s v. πρυτανεία; Hdt. i. 146.

The Delphic Oracle

and who knew the will of Heaven like Apollo, sole confidant of Zeus? [1]

Indeed this function of Apollo as Ἀρχηγέτης, or emigration leader, dates from prehistoric times, as is shown by the legend that the Dorian invasion was directed or sanctioned by Apollo.[2] This legend has a strong foundation in the fact that it best explains the constant close relations which, as we have seen, existed between Sparta and the Delphic Oracle.[3] Again, we have the legend of the Dryopians conquered by Heracles and made temple-slaves (ἱερόδουλοι) of Apollo, and afterwards brought as colonists to Messenia in the Peloponnesus.[4] Of similar import is the legend in Athenaeus [5] about Magnesia on the Meander, where the people were called "colonists of Delphi" (Δελφῶν ἄποικοι).

[1] Cf. Bouché-Leclercq, op. cit. iii. pp. 130–1. For Apollo as confidant of Zeus vid. supr. pp. 45–6.

[2] Vid. Pind. P. v. 69–73 :

> τῷ [καὶ] Λακεδαίμονι
> ἐν Ἄργει τε καὶ ζαθέᾳ Πύλῳ
> ἔνασσεν ἀλκάεντας Ἡρακλέος
> ἐκγόνους Αἰγιμίου τε,

"wherefore even for the sake of Lacedaemon he planteth the valiant descendants of Heracles and Aegimius in Argos and in hallowed Pytho."

[3] Vid. supr. p. 84, n. 6.

[4] Paus. iv. 34. 9. For the Dryopians of Parnassus vid. Ridgeway, op. cit. I. p. 104. R. maintains that they were neither Dorians nor Achaeans, but of an older race.

[5] p. 173 C : Μάγνητες οἱ ἐπὶ τῷ Μεανδρῳ ποταμῷ κατοικοῦντες ἱεροὶ τοῦ θεοῦ Δελφῶν ἄποικοι παρέχουσι τοῖς ἐπιδημοῦσι στέγην, ἅλας, ἔλαιον, ὄξος, ἔτι λύχνον, κλίνας, στρώματα, τραπέζας ; vid. Farnell, op. cit. iv. pp. 201, 376.

Political Influence of the Delphic Oracle

Finally, there is the legend—which gives another illustration of the ancient practice of dedicating a portion of. the captives taken in war to Delphic Apollo [1]—the legend which tells of the foundation of Colophon and the famous Oracle of Claros.[2] Manto, the daughter of Tiresias, the Theban seer, and other Thebans, being captured by the Epigoni, were consecrated to the Delphic god, who sent them out to found a colony in Asia Minor. It must be noted that this practice of devoting tithes of prisoners to the god is found only at Delphi in connexion with colonization.[3]

Of Pythian Apollo in this function of Ἀρχηγέτης in historic times the special spheres of activity were Libya, Italy, and Sicily. According to Herodotus,[4] the founding of Cyrene by the Theraeans was due to the persistent instructions of the Delphic Oracle.[5] Whether Grinus, king of Thera, consulted the Oracle on general matters,[6] or Battus [7] consulted it

[1] Apollo was invoked as helper in war under the title of Βοηδρόμιος, vid. Callim. Hymn. Ap. 69 ; Paus. ix. 17. 2 (πλησίον δὲ Ἀπόλλων τέ ἐστιν ἐπίκλησιν Βοηδρόμιος); vid. P.W. (s.v. Apollon), 45.

[2] Paus. vii. 3. i.

[3] Cf. Farnell, op. cit. iv. p. 201.

[4] For the founding of Cyrene vid. Hdt. iv. 150 ff.; Pind. P. iv. 63 ; Plut. De Pyth. Orac. xxii. xxvii. ; Paus. x. 15. 4.

[5] Acc. to Bury, "Hist. Gr." p. 116, the real reason for the departure of the emigrants from Thera was civil dissension between the older population, the Minyans, and the later Dorian settlers. The date of the founding of Cyrene is about 630 B.C.

[6] Hdt. iv. 150.

[7] His original name seems to have been Aristoteles. But

The Delphic Oracle

concerning his voice,[1] or the citizens of Thera regarding drought or some other trouble, the invariable response was that Battus should found a colony in " sheep-feeding Libya." Urged thus persistently, the people of Thera set about complying with the orders of Apollo. First Battus, with some of the Theraeans, settled on the little island, named Plataea, off the coast. This proving a failure, they applied once more in their distress to Delphi.[2] Reassured by the god, they now settled on the mainland opposite, at a place called Aziris, with beautiful hills on either side and a river flowing by.[3] Here they dwelt for six years, but left it at the persuasion of the Libyans for a place " suitable for Greeks to dwell in," and named Iraza.[4] Such is the story of the founding of the important colony of Cyrene. On this occasion the Oracle made a particularly happy choice, for the site of the city was one of the finest in the world, wondrously blest by nature,[5] so that it is not surprising that the city attained such wealth and eminence under the powerful dynasty of the Battiadae.[6]

after becoming king of Cyrene he took the title Battus, which apparently was the Libyan for " king," vid. Hdt. iv. 155; cf. Bury, " Hist. Gr." p. 116.

[1] Hdt. iv. 155; Pind. P. iv. 63; Plut. De Pyth. Orac. xxii.
[2] Hdt. iv. 157; Plut. De Pyth. Orac. xxvii.
[3] Hdt. ibid.   [4] Hdt. iv. 158.
[5] Vid. Hdt. iv. 157; Pind. P. iv. 56.
[6] Cf. Bury, " Hist. Gr." p. 116. The Oracle continued its watchful care over the colony. Hdt. (iv. 159) tells us that in the

Political Influence of the Delphic Oracle

Particularly interesting in this connexion is the history of Rhegium. Combining the statements of Strabo and Diodorus,[1] we see that the people of Chalcis in a season of dearth dedicated, in accordance with an oracle, a tithe of their number to Apollo. Those who were thus dedicated came to Delphi to inquire about a colony, and the god promised to give them a home in the Ausonian land. This story of the dedication to Apollo of tithes from among the Chalcidic population is particularly important, as it shows that the *ver sacrum*[2] was, as Dionysius of Halicarnassus maintained,[3] a Hellenic as well as an Italian custom. Tarentum,[4] also, and Croton[4] were founded under the guidance and encouragement of Pythian Apollo.

All the first Greek colonies in Sicily, according to Bury,[5] were founded by the Chalcidians under the auspices of Apollo. Naxos, the new city founded by the Chalcidians and the Ionians of the island of

---

reign of Battus III, the Delphic Oracle encouraged all the Greeks to sail to Libya and join the Cyrenaeans. The chief source of the wealth of Cyrene was the export of the silphium plant, which was valuable for medicinal purposes. The sale of silphium was a regal monopoly. On a Cyrenaean cup we have a scene depicting Arcesilaus II himself watching the plant being weighed and packed. Vid. Bury, " Hist. Gr." pp. 116–7.

[1] Strab. 257; Diod. viii. Fr. 23; the traditional date of its founding is 715 B.C.

[2] For the *ver sacrum* vid. Smith's " Dict. of Ant." ii. p. 939.

[3] i. 16.

[4] Paus. x. 10. 6; Strab. 262.   [5] " Hist. Gr." p. 98.

The Delphic Oracle

Naxos, was the first of these settlements—the first homestead of the Greeks in Sicily. To Apollo Archegetes an altar was erected on the spot where the Greeks first landed,[1] driven thither, it was said, by adverse winds in accordance with the dispensation of Apollo. So, too, Syracuse,[2] the earliest of the Dorian cities, and destined to be the greatest, was founded by Corinthian emigrants under the leadership of Archias and the sanction of Delphi.[3]

Sufficient examples have been adduced to show the important rôle which the Delphic Oracle played in the matter of colonization. We may now ask, How was the Oracle in a position to confer such services ? Whence did it gain its knowledge as to what places were suitable for the founding of colonies ? Here there is no need to resort to any hypothesis of a preternatural light, no necessity to resort to the *deus ex machina* of divine inspiration. The natural explanation is that the Delphic priests commanded a range of information such as no other body in antiquity enjoyed. They were in touch with all parts of the known world, Greek and barbarian alike. Envoys came con-

---

[1] Thuc. vi. 3. The traditional date of the founding of the city is 735 B.C.

[2] The date of its founding is 734 B.C.

[3] Vid. Suidas (quoted by Farnell, op. cit. iv. p. 376) : Ἀρχίας Συρακόσιος καὶ Μύσκελλος Ἀχαιος ἦκον ἐς Δελφοὺς ἐν τῷ αὐτῷ τοῦ χρόνου καὶ ἤτουν ἄρα ὑπὲρ ὧν ἔμελλον οἰκίζειν πόλεων φήμην ἀγαθὴν λαβεῖν . . . λέγει δὲ ἡ Πυθία χώρας καὶ πόλεως οἰκήτορα, κ.τ.λ. Cf. Strab. 380.

stantly to the Oracle, and we may feel sure that the
Delphic priests did not neglect the excellent opportunity of gaining knowledge which this fact afforded.
Delphi might be regarded, in modern phraseology,
as a great intelligence bureau, in communication
with all parts of the known world. Thus the
Pythian priests were in a unique position, com-
manding unique sources of information, and so,
when at times emigrant leaders came to consult
the Oracle, it displayed a knowledge of strange
places, of strange peoples and customs, which
seemed truly marvellous, and indeed worthy of the
omniscient Pythian god.

To what motives must we attribute this zeal on
the part of the Delphic priests? Doubtless they
had a genuine zeal for the spread of the Apolline
religion, which was most effectively done by
colonization. Yet it is probable that they were
not wholly disinterested. Indeed, we have some
positive proof of this. Over all the colonies, in
whose founding the Oracle had assisted, Delphi
maintained a right of suzerainty, which involved
certain practical demands. The cities owed, as a
mark of obedience and loyalty, tithes of their produce,[1] or, rather, its equivalent in gold—the famous
" golden harvest " ($\chi\rho\upsilon\sigma\sigma\hat{\upsilon}\nu$ $\theta\acute{\epsilon}\rho\sigma\varsigma$).[2] There was not,
however, a formal obligation to this effect, and very

[1] Cf. the epithet of Apollo $\Delta\epsilon\kappa\alpha\tau\eta\phi\acute{o}\rho\sigma\varsigma$, vid. Paus. i. 42. 5;
P.W. (s.v. Apollon), 47.
[2] Vid. Plut. De Pyth. Orac. xvi.: $\dot{\epsilon}\gamma\dot{\omega}$ $\delta\dot{\epsilon}$ $\kappa\alpha\dot{\iota}$ $M\upsilon\rho\iota\nu\alpha\acute{\iota}\upsilon\varsigma$

The Delphic Oracle

many of the colonies failed to carry out what should
have been, at any rate, a debt of gratitude. Three
cities, nevertheless, are cited as having been the
most faithful in observing this duty—Metapontum,
Myrina and Apollonia. And Apollo $Κερδῷος$ [1] knew
how to reward those who were not niggardly in his
service, just as he knew how to requite those who
through avarice refused his tribute.[2] At any rate,
the Delphic priests understood full well that the
spread of the Greek people by colonization under
the auspices of Pythian Apollo meant the spread
of his cult and the growth of his prestige, and
thus they could hope for an increase in the number
of his worshippers and in the number of the offerings " within the threshold of stone in rocky
Pytho." Yet, whatever may have been the
motives of its priesthood, the fact remains that the
Oracle, in thus encouraging the expansion of the
Hellenic race and directing the waves of colonization, conferred an incalculable service upon Greece.

$ἐπαινῶ$ $καὶ$ $’Απολλωνιάτας$, $θέρη$ $χρυσᾶ$ $δεῦρο$ $πέμψαντας$. The tribute
consisted apparently of golden ears of corn, cf. the coins of
Metapontum showing an ear of corn.

[1] Vid. *P.W.* (s.v. Apollon), 56.

[2] Cf. the story in Paus. (x. 11. 2), how Apollo bade the
Siphnians bring tithes to Delphi of the profits accruing from
their mines. When, however, they ceased out of avarice to
bring the tribute, the sea flowed in and covered the mines.
The second part of the story—that the sea covered the mines
—is true enough, for traces of them have been found at the
sea-bottom not far from the shore of the ancient Siphnos (modern
Siphno). Vid. Frazer, " Comm. Paus." x. 11. 2.

Political Influence of the Delphic Oracle

Section D : Pythian Apollo as Legislator

Another important sphere of Pythian Apollo's activity was that of legislator and source of public law.[1] In general, Apollo had a deep concern with law and its observance. Very important in this connexion are the name and history of the court at Athens known as " that at the Delphinium " (τὸ ἐπὶ Δελφινίῳ), " the Delphinium " being the temple of the Dolphin-god, Apollo. This court had special jurisdiction in cases where justification was claimed for confessed homicide. Even before the days of Solon the Athenian legal constitution conceded that homicide is sometimes justifiable—a fact which marked a momentous advance in criminal jurisprudence on the old-time legislation of the *Lex Talionis*. It is of first-rate importance, therefore, to note that such advance was associated with the legend of Apollo Δελφίνιος. Again, as we shall presently see, Apollo was intimately connected with the enfranchisement of slaves.

But it is especially to the Delphic shrine that we must look for Apollo's association with law. The Oracle seems to have been consulted occasionally in early as well as in later times as to the best mode of government, though probably such consultation was usually resorted to in cases of civil strife resulting in bloodshed.[2] The answer

[1] Vid. Farnell, op. cit. iv. pp. 197–200.

[2] Cf. Hdt. iv. 160–1. Cf. the case of the Corcyraeans, weary of civil strife, asking the Oracle of Dodona τίνι κα θεῶν ἢ ἡρώων

The Delphic Oracle

to such inquiries usually suggested a legislator or arbitrator—Zaleucus [1] to the Locrians, Demonax of Mantinea to the Cyrenaeans.[2] At times the Oracle gave vague hints as to the lines on which the legislation should run, for example, in the case of the well-known response given to the Megarians (asking in what manner they should be prosperous), " to take counsel with the majority " (μετὰ τῶν πλείστων βουλεύσασθαι).[3] And who were better qualified to make such suggestions than the Delphic priests,

θύοντες καὶ εὐχόμενοι ὁμονοοῖεν ἐπὶ τἀγαθόν, " to what god or hero offering sacrifice and prayer they might live in harmony unto good," vid. Farnell, op. cit. i. p. 40.

[1] Schol. Pind. O. xi. 17, quoting from Aristotle's Λοκρῶν πολιτεία (vid. Farnell, op. cit. iv. p. 197, note).

[2] Hdt. iv. 161. Apart from sending on request such occasional missionaries—and with these cf. Tyrtaeus, the Athenian, sent to the Spartans (Paus. iv. 15. 6 ; Diod. xv. 66), Epimenides, the Cretan, sent to purify Athens (Plut. Solon, xii. ; Paus. i. 14. 4 ; Grote, " Hist. Gr." iii. pp. 302–3)—the Delphic Oracle does not seem to have had any fixed representatives anywhere. The only exception is Sparta, where the four Pythii (or Poethii) were permanent officials (Hdt. vi. 57). The ἐξηγῆται Πυθόχρηστοι at Athens played only an insignificant rôle : their function was merely to watch ἀπὸ τῆς ἐσχάρας τοῦ ἀστραπαίου Διός, i.e. to watch for a certain meteorological sign— the flashing of lightning at a place called Harma, which was the signal for starting the *theoria*, or sacred embassy, to Delphi (vid. Strab. 404, and cf. Eur. Ion, 285 : ἀστραπαὶ Πύθιαι) ; yet Plato introduces them into his later ideal state (Legg. vi. 759 C). Other states merely sent envoys (θεωροί) on occasion to consult the Oracle.

[3] Paus. i. 43. 3. The exact words of the Oracle were : Μεγαρέας εὖ πράξειν ἢν μετὰ τῶν πλείστων βουλεύσωνται. The Megarians misinterpreted the oracle, thinking it to refer to the dead.

possessing as they did such opportunities of knowing local custom and requirements ?

But apart from such cases of general suggestions as to legislation, have we any cases of an actual code drafted by the Pythian god ? There was a strong tradition that the Spartan constitution of Lycurgus was dictated to him by the Pythia.[1] This oracular origin, however, for the constitution of Lycurgus is very doubtful. In the first place, the Spartans themselves, according to Herodotus, maintained that it was of Cretan origin—a statement which surprises us, considering the intimacy of the relations existing between Sparta and Delphi. Again, it is contrary to the method of the Oracle in historical times, which contented itself with vague general suggestions. Xenophon,[2] therefore, seems nearer the truth when he says that Lycurgus went to Delphi to ask the god whether it was better for Sparta to obey his laws. Lycurgus, then, merely

[1] Plato, Legg. 632 D ; Hdt. i. 65 (who, however, rather accepts the Cretan origin) ; Plut. Lyc. xxix. ; Strab. 482 ; cf. the legend that Minos got his code from Zeus (Plat. Legg. 632 D). Cf. also the story of Numa and the nymph Egeria (vid. Liv. i. 21 ; Plut. Numa, 13 ; Juv. iii. 12).

[2] Rep. Laced. viii. 5 : ἐλθών (sc. Λυκοῦργος) εἰς Δελφοὺς ἐπήρετο τὸν θεὸν εἰ λῷον καὶ ἄμεινον εἴη τῇ Σπάρτῃ πειθομένῃ οἷς αὐτὸς ἔθηκε νόμοις. That the Delphic Oracle merely gave its sanction to the code of laws already drawn up by Lycurgus would appear from Philostr. Apollon. of Tyana, viii. 7 : ἀφίκετο μὲν γὰρ ἐς τὸ ἱερὸν αὐτοῦ Λυκοῦργος ὁ ἐκ τῆς Σπάρτης, ἄρτι γεγραμμένων αὐτῷ τῶν νόμων οἷς ἡ Λακεδαίμων τέτακται, κ.τ.λ. (Cf. Cic. De Div. i. 43, § 96, "Lycurgus quidem . . . leges suas auctoritate Apollinis Delphici confirmavit.")

The Delphic Oracle

asked for Apollo's sanction for his legislation : the Spartan laws could in this sense be regarded as Πυθόχρηστοι νόμοι.[1] This, of course, would naturally give rise in later times to the story of divine inspiration. There is, however, a fragment of Tyrtaeus, preserved by Plutarch,[2] from which we gather that certain early kings who introduced reforms into Sparta " having heard Phoebus brought home from Pytho oracles of god and words of authority." That there is a large amount of truth in this is highly probable. We may be sure that each reformer or legislator would try to show a mandate from the Oracle, thereby investing his enactments with divine sanction.

An important question in this connexion (though indeed the question has as much a religious as a political bearing) is the relations of the Delphic Oracle with slavery. Greek religion in general in some ways served to ameliorate the hard lot of the slave, thus making for social progress. But no cult was so potent for good in this respect as that of Delphian Apollo. Though the enfranchisement of slaves is connected with other shrines,[3] with

[1] For the expression cf. Xen. Rep. Laced. viii. 5 (vid. L. and S. s.v. Πυθόχρηστος).

[2] Lyc. vi.:

> Φοίβου ἀκούσαντες Πυθωνόθεν οἴκαδ᾽ ἔνεικαν
> μαντείας τε θεοῦ καὶ τελέεντ᾽ ἔπεα.

[3] Cf. C.I.G. 1779a: ἀφίειτι Σάων ᾿Ατέαν ἐλεύθερον ἐναντία τῶ ᾿Ασκληπιῶ κὴ ᾿Απόλλωνος (inscr. from Thespiae). Cf. B.C.H. xvii. p. 361: ἀπέδοτο ᾿Αριστίων . . . τῶι ᾿Απόλλωνι τῶι Πυθίωι καὶ τῶι

Political Influence of the Delphic Oracle

Delphi are associated the most numerous examples.[1] The slave deposits with the god a certain sum—the sum, however, varying according to his age and accomplishments— which is to be paid over in the presence of witnesses to his former master. From the latter he is henceforth to be free, the god becoming the fictitious master, and guaranteeing the observance of his rights. The god, however, purchases the slave, not to retain him as a temple-slave (ἱερόδουλος), as sometimes happened in other circumstances, but to make him free. One example,[2] typical of the whole group of inscriptions, will serve to illustrate. " In the archonship of Pisilas, in the month of Amalius, Phalacrion, son of Sosicrates, on these conditions sold to Apollo a male slave, whose name was Dionysius, born in the house, at the price of 3½ minae of silver, according as Dionysius entrusted the god with the transaction of the sale, on condition that he should be free and immune from all seizure all his life,[3] doing whatsoever he pleases.[4] Surety according to law :

Ἀσκληπιῶι τῶι ἐν Ἀμφίσσαι . . . We find the manumission of slaves associated with Dionysus alone at Naupactus, *C.I.G.* 1756-7.

[1] 659 acts of enfranchisement have been found at Delphi. Vid. *B.C.H.* xx. p. 98.

[2] Vid. *B.C.H.* xvii. p. 346.

[3] ἐλεύθερος εἶμεν καὶ ἀνέφαπτος. Manumission at Delphi was really a sort of ἀνάθεσις, or dedication to the god. The slave became as regards liberty sacrosanct (ἱερὸς καὶ ἀνέφαπτος).

[4] Sometimes a clause is inserted here to the effect that, should anyone lay hands upon the manumitted slave for the purpose

The Delphic Oracle

Xenocrates, son of Calliteles, native of Lilaea. Witnesses: the priests Xenon, Athambus, and of the archons Cleodamus; private persons Carixenus, Callias, Agathon, Sosidamas."

Such in general is the nature of the transaction. In the main there is no mere legal fiction, for the god pays in each case the full market price, the owner certifies that payment has been made in full, and the slave is free. Sometimes, however, certain restrictions are included in the terms of sale, which bind the manumitted slave (ἀπελεύθερος) to certain obligations towards his former master. As has been already pointed out, the money wherewith the transaction is carried out comes from the slave himself—got together from his hard-earned savings. As a slave had no rights against his master, he was wise in thus entrusting the sale to the god. For, if he had given the money directly to his master, the latter might with perfect impunity have pocketed it, and retained the slave. But when he entrusted the sale to the god, immediately the whole transaction became invested with an element of sanctity, so that contravention of the terms of sale on the part of the original owner would have incurred the serious displeasure of the divinity.

Furthermore, it was to the interests of the Delphic authorities to see that the whole transaction was duly and legitimately carried out. Otherwise they

of re-enslaving him, the seller and surety are to maintain for the god the original terms of sale.

would have run the risk of spoiling a prosperous and, in all probability, a lucrative business. For, doubtless, the manumitted slave did not forget—was not permitted to forget—the author of his freedom. It must be distinctly understood, however, that the Delphic god was no abolitionist of slavery, for he himself maintained a number of slaves in connexion with the temple (ἱερόδουλοι).[1] Yet, in general, the Delphic Oracle in fostering the manumission of slaves and in helping to soften their hard lot[2] promoted a work which tended towards the advancement of Greece along the path of progress and humanity.

[1] The position of these temple-slaves, however, does not seem to have been a hard one; cf. Eur. Phoen. 202 ff., where the chorus consists of Phoenician maidens who have left " the Tyrian wave and have come as first-fruits to be slaves in the halls of Phoebus." Their lot is clearly a pleasant one : the service of Apollo is but a refined delight (cf. παρθένιον χλιδάν, ibid. 224). Such, too, is the position of Ion at Delphi. His life is but an alternation of " glorious toil " and " leisure the dearest unto men " (Eur. Ion, 131, 634).

[2] Cf. Paus. iii. 11. 8, where we see the Delphic Oracle persuading the Spartans to grant pardon to the rebel Helots, who had taken up a position on Mt. Ithome.

CHAPTER IV

INFLUENCE OF THE DELPHIC ORACLE ON RELIGION

SECTION A : FUNCTION OF THE ORACLE IN RELIGION IN GENERAL

IF the Delphic Oracle failed to effect a union in matters political, it succeeded amply in bringing about a union in matters religious. Delphi was the great Pan-Hellenic centre of religion. There was the " common hearth," [1] from whose sacred, " undying fire " [2] the other sanctuaries of Greece had their fires rekindled and reconsecrated [3]; there

[1] Κοινὴ ἑστία, Plut. Arist. xx., Ael. Var. Hist. iv. 6 (vid. infr. pp. 165–6).

[2] Cf. Plut. De E ap. Delph. ii. ; Aesch. Cho. 1037.

[3] This is the probable inference from the statement in Plut. (Arist. xx.), who says that pure fire was brought to Plataea from the " common hearth " of Delphi ; cf. (*B.C.H.* xviii. p. 87) an inscr. (dating prob. 97–96 B.C.) found in the Treasury of the Athenians. In it is mentioned how a certain Iphicrates escorted the sacred tripod from Delphi, together with the " fire-bringing priestess " (ἔλαβε τὸν ἱερὸν τρίποδα ἐκ Δελφῶν καὶ ἀπεκόμισε, καὶ τὴν πυρφόρον ἤγαγεν Ἰφικράτης Ἐπιστράτου Ἀθηναῖος). It is not certain what is the exact reference. There is a clue, however, in Philostratus, Heroica (quoted *B.C.H.* xviii. p. 89, Louis Couve), where there is an analogous ceremony mentioned in regard to Lemnos. Every year the island was purified in view of the action of the Lemnian women of old. All the fires were extinguished, and

Influence of the Delphic Oracle on Religion

was the " common tripod of Greece," [1] to which all Greeks resorted seeking light on important matters of religious legislation. " For Apollo of Delphi," says Plato, " will remain the most important, the noblest, and the chiefest acts of legislation . . . the erection of temples, and the appointment of sacrifices and other ceremonies in honour of gods and demi-gods and heroes, and again the modes of burial of the dead, and all the observances which we must adopt to propitiate the denizens of the other world. . . . For it is this god, I presume, expounding from his seat on the Omphalos at the earth's centre who is the national expositor on such matters." [2]   And in the *Laws* [3] he lays it down

fresh fire was brought from Delos by sacred envoys. Some such ceremony must be referred to here. A tripod was brought to Delphi by a sacred embassy, of which Iphicrates was head, and reconsecrated at some Delphic festival, perhaps the festival of the Heraclea. This was probably the feast of purification of the Delphic tripod, sullied by the contact of Heracles, who had struggled for it against Apollo. So Mommsen, " Delphika," p. 322 : " Heracles hatte den Dreifuss angetastet . . . so dass das heiligste aller Geräte wohl gar mit Staub und Schweiss bisudelt worden ; da war denn eine Reconsecration des Dreifuss nötig." Iphicrates would have accompanied the priestess who was to preside at the sacrifice and bring back the sacred fire to rekindle the fire in the Athenian sanctuary. With the expression ἡ πυρφόρος cf. ὁ πυρφόρος, the priest who accompanied the Lacedaemonian army, keeping the sacred fire, which was never allowed to go out, vid. Xen. Rep. Laced. xiii. 2, (cf. L. and S. s.v. πυρφόρος).

[1] τρίποδα κοινὸν Ἑλλάδος (Eur. Ion, 366).
[2] Rep. 427 B–C.   [3] 738 C.

The Delphic Oracle

as an axiom that no legislator is to alter any cult, whether native or exotic, which has received the approbation of the Oracles of Delphi, Dodona, or Zeus Ammon.

That the Delphic Oracle should play such an important rôle in religious matters is quite natural. In matters of religious difficulty what safer guide could be found than Pythian Apollo, who knew and could disclose the secrets of the unseen world? We find the statement of Plato, that the god at Delphi was the "national expositor" in matters of religion, borne out by numerous examples. Let us take a few instances out of many. The Ionians consult the Oracle regarding the common worship of Poseidon : they are bidden to take models of the ancient ancestral altars of Helice.[1] The Greeks after the victory at Plataea ask about the manner of sacrifice : they are told to erect in Plataea an altar to "Zeus of Freedom" (Ζεὺς Ἐλευθέριος).[2] The Athenians are troubled by some meteoric phenomenon : the Oracle enjoins upon them to sacrifice with good omens to all the Olympian deities (first in the list being "Zeus most high"), to make public offerings in the streets to Apollo "of the ways" (Ἀγυιεύς), Leto, Artemis, and Dionysus, and, above all, to remember their native hero and their dead.[3]

[1] Diod. xv. 49.
[2] Plut. Arist. xx.; cf. Strab. 412; Paus. ix. 2. 5; C.I.G. 1672.
[3] Dem. Macart. 1072: ἐπερωτᾷ ὁ δῆμος ὁ Ἀθηναίων περὶ τοῦ σημείου

Influence of the Delphic Oracle on Religion

Occasionally the Oracle seems to air its ritualistic lore by bidding a community worship some unknown or unfamiliar divinity. The Epidaurians, when consulting it on an occasion of dearth, are bidden to erect statues of Damia and Auxesia.[1] Sometimes, perhaps, its motive in thus introducing some new cult, or reviving an obsolete one, was by way of experiment: the old prescription had lost its efficacy, and the Oracle wished to try that of the new.

Generally speaking, in religious matters the Delphic Oracle did not encourage innovations. Its general tendency is illustrated by the well-known statement of Xenophon:[2] consultants are advised to follow the custom of each particular state. This policy of the Oracle in religious matters is quite in harmony with its policy in matters political; for,

τοῦ ἐν τῷ οὐρανῷ γενομένου . . . συμφέρει Ἀθηναίοις περὶ τοῦ σημείου τοῦ ἐν τῷ οὐρανῷ γενομένου θύοντας καλλιερεῖν Διὶ ὑπάτῳ Ἀθηνᾷ ὑπάτῃ, Ἡρακλεῖ, Ἀπόλλωνι σωτῆρι, καὶ ἀποπέμπειν ἀμφὶ ὀνήσει, κ.τ.λ.

[1] Htd. v. 82. Auxesia is clearly the " goddess of increase," from √ of αὐξάνω which is prob. FEΞ with a prefixed; cf. Skt. *vakshami* (*cresco*), Germ. *wachsen*, Eng. *wax*. (Lat. *augere* is prob. from a different √. Acc. to Curtius it is from √ΤΓ which appears in ὑγιής.) Damia (like Deo) is probably only another form of Demeter. The divinities, therefore, to be honoured were the " Corn-Mother " (name Demeter being best connected with δηαί, Cretan form of ζειαί, " barley ") and the " goddess of increase "—a natural prescription for ἀφορία.

[2] Mem. iv. 3. 16: ὁρᾷς γὰρ ὅτι ὁ ἐν Δελφοῖς θεός, ὅταν τις αὐτὸν ἐπερωτᾷ πῶς ἂν τοῖς θεοῖς χαρίζοιτο, ἀποκρίνεται Νόμῳ Πόλεως. Cf. ibid. iv. 3: ἥ τε γὰρ Πυθία νόμῳ πόλεως ἀναιρεῖ ποιοῦντας εὐσεβῶς ἂν ποιεῖν.

The Delphic Oracle

as we have seen, it did not show any marked political programme. To what motive was this tolerance in religion due ? By some [1] it has been regarded as showing a spirit of broad-mindedness, which at such an early age was remarkable. This may be true, but we must not exclude the possibility that the Delphic priests were swayed by mixed motives. Their policy may have been due partly to conservative instincts, which clung tenaciously to tradition, partly to prudential considerations. They knew that to discourage local tradition would inevitably lead to religious quarrels, which would prove detrimental to their own interests. Nor does the Oracle seem to have arrogated to itself the right of disciplinary jurisdiction over the ministers of other cults—not but that it got at times an opportunity of doing so. [2]

[1] Cf. F. W. H. Myers, " Essays," p. 46.

[2] Cf. Hdt. vi. 135—the case of Timo, priestess of the infernal goddesses at Paros, who was accused of revealing to Miltiades certain mysteries, which were ἐς ἄρσενα γόνον ἄρρητα. Cf. Plut. De Pyth. Orac. xx.—the case of a priest of Heracles Misogynist, who had violated his vow of chastity. Both were acquitted by the Oracle, whose plea was that the former case was due to the working of Fate, the latter to the exigencies of human nature (ἅπαντα τἀναγκαῖα συγχωρεῖ θεός). The action of the Oracle in these two cases is, as we shall see, probably due to an ethical advance at Delphi. Contrast its action in case of the priestess of Artemis, whom it ordered to be sacrificed to the offended goddess (Paus. vii. 19. 2). Vid. infr. p. 129.

Influence of the Delphic Oracle on Religion

Section B : Pythian Apollo as Religious Propagandist

In regard to religious cults generally, the Delphic Oracle does not seem to have had any definite propagandist programme. Of course there was no necessity of propagating the worship of Apollo, which was already deeply rooted in Greece from the earliest times, and which was sufficiently diffused by colonization. Colonies, which almost invariably were sent out, or at least sanctioned, by the Oracle, were connected with it by cult relations, and doubtless its priests let slip no opportunity of inculcating the necessity of maintaining a spirit of loyalty and filial devotion. But except in this very limited sense, we cannot speak of the Delphic priesthood as preaching the worship of Apollo. There are two cults, however, towards which the Oracle showed a decided leaning, and whose growth it sought zealously to foster.[1] These are the cults of Dionysus and of heroes.

Of Delphic enthusiasm for the spread of the Dionysiac worship we have abundant proof. At home Dionysus becomes the cult brother of Apollo, sharing his epithets and his worship, excluded from nothing save only the oracular prerogative.[2] Abroad his worship is propagated by

---

[1] Divinities thus introduced to a community were known as θεοὶ Πυθόχρηστοι. Cf. Πυθόχρηστοι νόμοι, p. 108 (supr.) and ibid. n. 1 ; also ἐξηγῆται Πυθόχρηστοι, p. 106, n. 2.

[2] Vid. chap. i. pp. 33–4.

The Delphic Oracle

Delphic influence at Magnesia (on the Maeander),[1] at Lesbos,[2] at Athens,[3] at Sicyon,[4] at Patrae,[5] at Potniae,[6] at Sparta,[7] at Peiraeus,[8] at Corinth,[9] and many other places. The " Artists of Dionysus " (τεχνῖται Διονύσου)[10]—those associations of theatrical artists, musicians and actors—always received the warmest approbation and protection of the Pythian shrine. In an inscription [11] they are spoken of as " honoured by gods and kings and all Greeks, who have given them all the rights of inviolability and personal safety . . . in accordance with the oracles of Apollo." In a Hymn to Apollo,[12] recently discovered at Delphi, they are called the " great, holy, thyrsus-smitten band [13] of artists of Dionysus." They are honoured by the Amphictyonic Council with a decree granting them the privileges of ἀσυλία and ἀτέλεια.[14]

How far the priests were actuated by inner conviction in this matter it is impossible to tell. Per-

---

[1] Vid. Farnell, op. cit. v. p. 281.   [2] Paus. x. 19. 3.
[3] Paus. i. 2. 5 ; Dem. Meid. § 52.   [4] Paus. ii. 7. 6.
[5] Paus. vii. 19. 6-10.   [6] Paus. ix. 8. 1.
[7] Paus. iii. 13. 7.
[8] Vid. Farnell, op. cit. v. p. 311 n
[9] Paus. ii. 2. 7.
[10] They were also called οἱ περὶ τὸν Διόνυσον τεχνῖται, C.I.G. 3067 ; cf. Dem. 401.
[11] C.I.G. 3067.   [12] B.C.H. xviii. p. 352.
[13] The original word is undecipherable; ἔσμος is suggested by a writer (H. Weil) in B.C.H. (ibid.)
[14] Vid. Farnell, op. cit. iv. p. 311. For a very full list of references to the τεχνῖται vid. op. cit. v. pp. 310-13.

Influence of the Delphic Oracle on Religion

haps they were genuinely fired with some of the
enthusiasm for the cult of the son of Semele, which
at an early period had taken possession of Greece.
But perhaps, too, as has been already suggested,
their devotion to Dionysus is sufficiently accounted
for by the strong position which Dionysus apparently had won before his arrival at Delphi. The
Apolline priesthood with their wonted sagacity saw
that the new divinity had come to be a power in
Greece, and so thought well to buy off the opposition of a dangerous rival by sharing with him the
honours of Pythian Apollo.[1]

But, though the Delphic Oracle was so devoted
to the Dionysiac worship, there is no proof that it was
enthusiastic for the spread of the Demeter cult
in general or of the Attic mysteries in particular.
There is, it is true, a decree of the Amphictyonic
Council, which extols the past glory of Athens,
declaring it to be the first beginning of all blessings
among men, and the earliest home of law and culture, by having introduced the mysteries and
thereby proclaimed to men that the chiefest blessing
is in fellowship and trust.[2] But it must be remembered that this is a mere secular decree, not
an oracular utterance. There is, however, one
instance where the Oracle counsels the giving of
first-fruits (ἀπαρχαί) to Demeter and Kore, the
Eleusinian divinities.[3] But this, of course, may

---

[1] Vid. supr. i. pp. 33–4.　[2] B.C.H. xxiv. (1900), p. 96.
[3] Vid. Dittenb. Syll. 13 (quoted by Farnell, op. cit. iii. p. 346),

The Delphic Oracle

have been merely a response to a question put by Athenians on the occasion of a bad harvest—a not infrequent cause of consultation.[1] Then it would naturally occur to the Oracle to advise them to pay more attention to the worship of Demeter or Kore. Consequently, the statement in the inscription does not really prove any fostering or encouragement of the Eleusinian mysteries.

The other cult towards which the Delphic Oracle showed a decided leaning was that of heroes—a department in Greek religion of which it took over the supreme control. It is true, of course, that certain hero-cults may have been prior to the coming of Apollo. But from the seventh century B.C. till the time of Alexander the Great, it seems to have been the rule that no mortal should receive divine honours, or even " heroic " honours,[2] after

inscr. found at Eleusis, dating from the fifth century B.C. Cf. the cult of Κόρη Πυθόχρηστος at Erythrae. Vid. Dittenb. Syll. 370, l. 90: Δήμητρος καὶ Κόρης Πυθοχρήστου (quoted by Farnell, op. cit. iii. p. 341). Farnell, however (op. cit. iv. p. 206 note) points out that it is not certain that this cult at Erythrae was Πυθόχρηστος.

[1] Cf. Plut. De Def. Orac. xlvi.; Hdt. v. 82 (where the Pythia suggested the cult of Damia and Auxesia as a remedy against ἀφορία, vid. supr. p. 115, n. 1); Paus. viii. 42. 5–6, where the Oracle was consulted by the Phigalians of Arcadia on the occasion of dearth : they were bidden to appease the wrath of Deo (that is, Demeter) by libations and divine honours :

> Ἀρκάδες Ἀζᾶνες βαλανηφάγοι, οἳ Φιγάλειαν
> νάσσασθ᾽, ἱππολεχοῦς Δηοῦς κρυπτήριον ἄντρον,
> ἥκετε πευσόμενοι λιμοῦ λύσιν ἀλγινόεντος, κ.τ.λ.

[2] We must distinguish between apotheosis proper and " heroization." By the former a mortal gained access to

120

his death, unless with the sanction of the Oracle. Plato's words,[1] referred to at the beginning of this chapter, would seem to imply this. But how far this is merely a statement of what should be observed in the ideal state or of what was the rule in actual practice we cannot say with certainty. It seems strange that the Oracle—whose authority rested purely on the influence of its prestige without any coercive means at its disposal—should have arrogated to itself such rights. It seems strange, too, that states which so passionately loved local autonomy should have tolerated what seemed an infringement of their own rights. We may explain all this, however, by parallelism with the canonization of saints in the Roman Catholic Church. Just as only those are accepted as Saints whom the Church has authoritatively declared such, so, too, in ancient Greece, those alone could receive honours whom the Oracle had raised to the heroic dignity. Indeed, we find so many examples of Delphic ruling in this matter, that it seems probable that for at least the period of Greek independence the statement of Plato expresses the general truth.

In this matter of " heroization " the Delphic god was no respecter of persons : men of every race,

Olympus, as in the case of Dionysus, Asclepius, Heracles. Olympus, however, was not accessible to *heroes*, who are merely endowed with certain powers, which the ordinary dead have not. The Dioscuri, who are alternately gods and heroes, form a transition between the two classes.

[1] Rep. 427 B–C. Cf. Farnell, op cit. iv. pp. 206–7.

The Delphic Oracle

profession, and rank were deemed eligible for heroic honours. And so we find the cults of heroes of epic fame, heroes (or heroines) of agriculture, founders of colonies, warriors, statesmen, athletes—all encouraged or instituted by the Pythian shrine. Let us cite a few examples. The Mantineans are bidden by the Oracle to fetch from Maenalus to their own " lovely town " the bones of Arcas, " eponym of all Arcadians," and there " make unto him a precinct and sacrifices." [1] The Lacedaemonians, at the bidding of Pythian Apollo, convey from Helice, the ancient capital of Achaea, the bones of Tisamenus, who had been slain in battle against the Heraclidae, and bury them at Sparta.[2] The Orchomenians, consulting the Oracle on the occasion of a plague, are bidden to bring back the bones of Hesiod from the land of Naupactus to the land of Orchomenus.[3] On another occasion being terrified by a spectre which ravages the country, they are ordered by the Oracle to seek out the remains of Actaeon and bury them and make a statue to him.[4] The Lacedaemonians are told that if they

[1] Vid. Paus. viii. 9. 3–4: ἔστι δὲ Μαιναλίη δυσχείμερος, ἔνθα τε κεῖται | Ἀρκας, κ.τ.λ.

[2] Vid. Paus. vii. 1. 8. The tomb of Tisamenus was still extant in the time of Pausanias, who says that near it the Spartan public dinner (τὰ Φειδίτια) used to be held.

[3] Paus. ix. 38. 4. It is noteworthy that hero-cults were propagated by the Oracle usually when consulted on occasion of plague (λοιμός) or dearth (ἀφορία, ἀκαρπία).

[4] Paus. ix. 38. 5.

Influence of the Delphic Oracle on Religion

wish to be victorious over the Tegeans they must first bring back from Tegea the bones of Orestes, son of Agamemnon.[1] The Messenians at the bidding of the Oracle bring from Rhodes to Messenia the bones of their hero, Aristomenes.[2] The Athenians consulting the Oracle after Marathon regarding a certain mysterious figure, which had wrought prodigies of valour in the battle and then disappeared, get a response to the effect that they must honour the hero Echetlaeus.[3] The Oracle bids the Boeotians consulting it on the occasion of drought to get the cure from Trophonius.[4] Clisthenes goes to Delphi and asks if he is to drive out from Sicyon the hero Adrastus : he is sternly forbidden by the Oracle to do so, which declares that Adrastus indeed is king of the Sicyonians, but he their oppressor.[5] Before the battle of Plataea the Oracle bids the Athenians sacrifice to seven tutelary heroes ('Αρχηγέται) of the place.[6] The ten new tribes at Athens instituted by Clisthenes receive their names from the list of indigenous heroes furnished by the Oracle.[7]

But the Oracle was not content with bestowing

[1] Hdt. i. 67.   [2] Paus. iv. 32. 3.
[3] Paus. i. 32. 5.   [4] Paus. ix. 40. 1.
[5] Hdt. v. 67: Ἄδρηστον μὲν εἶναι Σικυωνίων βασιλέα, ἐκεῖνον δὲ λευστῆρα. Vid. supr. pp. 91–2.
[6] Plut. Aristid. xi.
[7] Pollux, Onomast. viii. 110: ἐκ πολλῶν ὀνομάτων ἐλομένου τὰ παλαιὰ τοῦ Πυθίου (quoted by Bouché-Leclercq, op. cit. iii. p. 141).

The Delphic Oracle

heroic honours on mere epic figures of the distant past ; it decreed them also to persons of much more recent celebrity. It began by bestowing almost divine honours upon legislators [1] or other men of genius [2] : it ended with the apotheosis of athletes ! Seized with that infatuation for athletics which breaks out at times in the history of every country, it went the length of giving heroic honours to athletes, some of them of doubtful reputation and suspicious renown.[3] The story of Cleomedes [4] is well known. This redoubtable champion was boxing with Iccus, an Epidaurian, and killed him. Condemned by the umpires for foul play he lost the prize and went mad through grief. Returning to his native Astypalaea he pulled down the props which supported the roof of a school full of children, all of whom were killed. Pelted with stones by the townsfolk he fled for refuge to

[1] Cf. the famous words addressed to Lycurgus by the Pythia (Hdt. i. 65) : διζῶ ἤ σε θεὸν μαντεύσομαι, ἢ ἄνθρωπον· | ἀλλ' ἔτι καὶ μᾶλλον θεὸν ἔλπομαι, ὦ Λυκόοργε, " I am in doubt whether I shall pronounce thee god or man, but rather god, Lycurgus." This response is referred to by Philostr. Apollon. of Tyana, viii. 7.

[2] Cf. the statement of Paus. (ix. 23. 3) that the Pythia ordered the Delphians to give Pindar an equal share in all the first-fruits they offered to Apollo : . . . ἡ Πυθία ἀνειποῦσα Δελφοῖς ὁπόσων ἀνήρχοντο τῷ Ἀπόλλωνι μοῖραν καὶ Πινδάρῳ τὴν ἴσην ἁπάντων νέμειν. Vid. supr. p. 77.

[3] Diog. Laert. v. 91, tells the story of the Pythia who, having decreed a sort of apotheosis to Heraclides Ponticus obtained by intrigue, was soon after bitten by a serpent in the adytum and died from the effects of the wound.

[4] Paus. vi. 9. 6–9. Cf. the story of Theagenes, Paus. vi. 11.

the sanctuary of Athene. He stepped into a chest
and drew down the lid, which could not again be
opened. At last the chest was broken open, but
lo! there was no Cleomedes! They sent men to
Delphi to learn what had become of him, and the
Pythia replied : " Last of the heroes is Cleomedes
of Astypalaea. Him do ye honour with sacrifices as
no longer a mortal." Such was " the last of the
heroes " ! The list was not closed a moment too soon.

What was the motive of this attitude of the
Oracle towards hero-worship ? Hero-worship was
characteristically Greek : it was in perfect accordance with the Hellenic spirit, which tended towards
the glorification of man. The tendency of the
Greek imagination, on the other hand, was to divest
its gods of attributes which transcended human
understanding. Thus it is that even the three
great rulers of the universe—Zeus, Poseidon, and
Hades—are no very imposing figures. Aeschylus
indeed invested his gods with a sublimity which
savours more of the Oriental than the Hellenic.
Yet, on the whole, it is true that the Greek divinities
were but glorified, idealized types of humanity. To
the Greek, then, the gulf which separated the divine
from the human nature was not immeasurable.
And so it is not surprising that we find in Greek
religion so many mortals " raised to the skies."
But yet, some deeper causes than this must be
sought. In the religion of Dionysus, which at an
early date became so intimately connected with

The Delphic Oracle

that of Apollo, were embodied two important doctrines—so extensively propagated by the Orphic mysticism—the doctrines of the immortality of the soul, and the possibility of a life of happiness beyond the grave.[1] Now the Pythian priests seem to have been influenced by this doctrine, for the Delphians themselves cultivated hero-worship,[2] and we see the Oracle inculcating upon the Athenians the necessity of ritual observance towards the dead.[3]

Furthermore, the Delphic priests may have been

[1] Vid. Burnet, " Gr. Philos." pt. i. pp. 31–2. Cf. Miss Harrison, " Proleg." p. 476 : " Orpheus retained the old Bacchic faith that man might become God, but he sought to obtain that Godhead not by physical intoxication, but by spiritual ecstasy —by abstinence and rites of purification. The cardinal doctrine of the Orphic religion was the possibility of attaining divine life. The great contribution which the religion of Dionysus brought was the hope of immortality it brought. Perfect purity issuing in the divinity is the key-note of the Orphic faith." The Orphic teachings must have been well known at Delphi. It is noteworthy that Orpheus was a conspicuous figure in the famous painting by Polygnotus (in the Lesche of the Cnidians) of Odysseus' descent to the lower world. For this painting vid. infr. p. 149.

[2] Paus. (x. 24. 6) tells us that the Delphians annually offered sacrifice to Neoptolemus as a hero : . . . καὶ οἱ (i.e. Νεοπτολέμῳ) κατὰ ἔτος ἐναγίζουσιν οἱ Δελφοί. They had also their native heroes, Phylacus and Autonous, who were thought to have defended the shrine of Apollo against the Persian invaders, 480 B.C. Vid. Hdt. viii. 39 : τούτους δὲ τοὺς δύο Δελφοὶ λέγουσιν εἶναι ἐπιχωρίους ἥρωας, Φύλακόν τε καὶ Αὐτόνοον. We shall find Phylacus figuring also in the legendary account of the Gallic invasion of Delphi, 279 B.C. Vid. infr. p. 171.

[3] Dem. Macart. 1072 : τοῖς ἀποφθιμένοις ἐν ἱκνουμένᾳ ἀμέρᾳ τελεῖν τοὺς ποθίκοντας καττὰ ἀγημένα. Vid. supr. p. 114.

genuinely convinced that this encouragement of tomb-ritual made for the stability of family life, and consequently for the stability of the state. They may have felt that to foster in the family a belief in and a worship of ever-present, powerful beings, who could make or mar its prosperity, tended towards the advancement, spiritual and material, of the social unit and consequently of society in general. Finally, it cannot have escaped them that it made considerably for the prestige of Pythian Apollo to have a number of cults propagated at his bidding, or at least with his sanction, which would naturally bind men more closely to the god of the great central sanctuary. Some such may have been the reasons which inclined the Delphic priests so strongly towards hero-worship.

SECTION C : THE ORACLE AND HUMAN SACRIFICE

Yet, wise and beneficent on the whole as was the religious administration of Delphi, there attaches, at least to the earlier period of its history, one great blot—the fact of its counselling and encouraging human sacrifice. Though human sacrifice was regarded, at least by the Greeks of the fifth century B.C., as something impious and barbaric,[1] yet, that it prevailed in ancient Greece [2] is proved by numerous

[1] Plat. Minos, 315 B: ἡμῖν μὲν οὐ νόμος ἐστὶν ἀνθρώπους θύειν ἀλλ᾽ ἀνόσιον.

[2] That human sacrifice prevailed in the Mycenaean Age is the probable conclusion of Ridgeway, " Early Age of Greece," I. p. 7.

The Delphic Oracle

legends. With the advance of civilization, however, the old savage ritual became modified, and
animals were substituted for the earlier human
victims.[1] Yet even in later times there were some
survivals of the ancient custom. Human sacrifice
seems to have survived in all its revolting horrors
to the time of Pausanias in connexion with the
Arcadian worship of Zeus on Mt. Lycaeus.[2] At
Orchomenus in Boeotia the priest of Dionysus
Laphystius (i.e. " the devourer," from λαφύσσειν,
" devour ") every year at the festival of the Agrionia
pursued with a drawn sword the maidens of the
Minyan stock, known as the "Oleae," and within
Plutarch's memory had actually slain one.[3] Plutarch
tells us also that the prophet forced Themistocles to
sacrifice the Persian captives to Dionysus Omestes.[4]
Diodorus [5] states that there was human sacrifice to
Kronos at Rhodes.[6]

[1] Eustath. ii. p. 331 (quoted by Farnell, op. cit. ii. p. 565).
For the substitution of goats for boys as sacrifices to Dionysus
at Potniae vid. Paus. ix. 8. 2. Cf. also the substitution of a
stag for a maiden in the ritual of Athene at Laodicea, vid.
Farnell, op. cit. p. 383 (quoting Porphyry, De Abstin. ii. 56).
Here, however, " Athene " seems an error for "Artemis."

[2] viii. 38. Cf. Euseb. Pr. Ev. iv. 16. 10.

[3] Quaest. Gr. xxxviii. The same writer (Pelop. xxi.) states
that the dream of Pelopidas was nearly fulfilled, which bade him
sacrifice a maiden to the Λευκτρίδες κόραι. Many of the Council
favoured its fulfilment, till chance offered a lucky substitute.

[4] Them. xiii.: ἐκέλευσε (sc. ὁ μάντις) τῶν νεανίσκων κατάρξασθαι,
κα καθιερῶσαι πάντας 'Ωμηστῇ Διονύσῳ προσευξάμενον.

[5] xiii. 86.

[6] At Athens in the festival of the Thargelia (a festival of

Influence of the Delphic Oracle on Religion

Of Delphi's sanctioning human sacrifice we have many proofs in legend. Let us cite a few examples. The Athenians, distressed by a plague owing to the murder of Androgeos, son of Minos, sought a remedy from Pythian Apollo : they were bidden to send annually a tribute of seven youths and seven maidens to be sacrificed in Crete.[1] The people of Potniae consulted the Oracle concerning a pestilence which fell upon the land as a consequence of their having slain the priest of Dionysus : they were bidden to sacrifice a boy in the bloom of youth.[2] The people of Aroe, Anthea, and Messatis (in Achaea) consulted the Oracle concerning the guilt-stained priestess of Artemis : they were told to sacrifice the priestess and her paramour and annually sacrifice a youth and a maiden.[3] A ruler of Haliartus consulted the Delphic god as to how he should find water in the land : the god commanded him to slay the first person he should meet on his return.[4] Menoeceus, son of Creon of Thebes, voluntarily slew himself in obedience to the Delphic Oracle when Polynices and his army came before Argos.[5]

Apollo and Artemis) two human " scapegoats " (καθάρματα, *piacula*), who were probably criminals, were sacrificed in a sort of religious execution. (Vid. Farnell, op. cit. iv. p. 268 ff.) We are not certain that the victims were killed : only late writers assert that. But the ritual points to original human sacrifice.

[1] Vid. Plut. Thes. xv. ; Euseb. Pr. Ev. v. 18–9.
[2] Paus. ix. 8. 1.   [3] Paus. vii. 19. 4.
[4] Paus. ix. 33. 4.   [5] Paus. ix. 25. 1.

The Delphic Oracle

All these instances are of course mere myths, but myths point to facts. And we have one example from the early historical period—the time of the First Messenian War. The Messenians, harassed in war, consulted the Oracle : they were advised to sacrifice " with nocturnal slaughter a spotless maiden chosen by lot, of the blood of the Aepytids, to the gods below." [1] There seems no reason for doubting the authenticity of this response.

How is it that the Delphic priests, in many respects so enlightened, should have sanctioned such a custom ? We may answer, in the first place, that Delphi was probably no worse in this respect than other oracle-centres. According to Dionysius of Halicarnassus,[2] there was an ancient oracle preserved at Dodona prescribing human sacrifice in the Italian worship of Jupiter and Saturn. In the ritual of Brauronian Artemis the goat which was sacrificed to the goddess was but a substitute for a maiden, whose sacrifice was enjoined by an oracle as a remedy for a plague.[3] Plutarch tells how Pherecydes was slain by the Spartans, and his skin preserved by the kings " in accordance with a certain oracle." [4]

[1] Paus. iv. 9. 4. Cf. Euseb. Pr. Ev. v. 27: παρθένον Αἰπυτίδα κλῆρος καλεῖ ἥντινα δοίης | δαίμοσι νερτερίοις, καί κεν σώσειας Ἰθώμην.

[2] Ant. Rom. i. 19. Cf. Farnell, op. cit. iv. p. 209. Cf. the story of Coresus and Callirhoe (Paus. vii. 21), according to which the oracle of Dodona ordained that Coresus should sacrifice Callirhoe or some one who would be willing to die for her.

[3] Eustath. ii. p. 331 (quoted by Farnell, op. cit. ii. p. 565).

[4] Pelop. xxi.

Influence of the Delphic Oracle on Religion

Again, the Delphic priests, with that conservatism which sometimes clings to outworn forms, no matter how unreasonable, might have been inclined to adhere to the old ceremonial : it is the *prophet* who forces upon Themistocles the sacrifice of the Persian captives to Dionysus Omestes.[1] And so in times of great distress the priest or prophet, like another Calchas, might demand that the wrath of the offended deity be appeased by the sacrifice of an Iphigenia.

[1] Them. xxi.

CHAPTER V

THE INFLUENCE OF THE DELPHIC ORACLE
ON MORALITY

SECTION A : ETHICAL EVOLUTION AT DELPHI

IN estimating the influence of the Delphic Oracle upon morality we should do well to follow one of the Oracle's wisest maxims, " Nothing to excess " (Μηδὲν ἄγαν). We must avoid the view which regards Delphi as a great missionary centre, whose priests are inspired teachers with an advanced dogma and a definite mission, and equally that view which would regard the Oracle and all its doings as meriting reprobation. The truth is that in this matter as in others the Oracle had its virtues and its faults, but on the whole its influence seems to have been for good. We have, of course, to rely mainly on the utterances of the Oracle (quoted by the writers of antiquity),[1] whose authenticity is

[1] Set collections of oracles existed apparently in ancient times. Cf. Eur. Fr. 629 (ed. Nauck, Teubner): εἰσὶν γὰρ, εἰσι διφθέραι μελαγγραφεῖς | πολλῶν γέμουσαι Λοξίου γηρυμάτων, " Verily there are dark-written tablets replete with many an utterance of Loxias." According to Cic. De Div. i. 19, § 37, Chrysippus " collected innumerable oracles." So, too, Nicander of Colophon was said to have composed a work, περὶ χρηστηρίων πάντων. We find him honoured with a decree declaring him " proxenus "

Influence of the Delphic Oracle on Morality

always more or less problematic. Taking these
utterances such as they are, we must recognize a
growth in the Oracle's ethical ideas—a gradual
transition from the old-time barbarous code, which
could sanction human sacrifice, to a more elevated
and more reasonable standpoint. We can distinguish three stages in this ethical evolution. The
first stage recognized only what may be called
social or extrinsic morality—that morality which
had reference only to the *forum externum*, taking
cognizance only of the external act. The internal
act of wrong-doing—in which the essence of malice
consists—gods and men ignored or condoned, but
the external act, whether voluntary or involuntary,
might be punished with a terrible vengeance.
Such was the morality of ancient Greece.[1] This
fact explains many things in antiquity, which are
utterly repugnant to modern ethical ideas. It explains the whole plot of the *Oedipus Tyrannus*.

of Delphi in the last quarter of the third cent. B.C. Vid.
B.C.H. vi. (1882), p. 217 ff. Mnaseas of Patrae also made a
collection of Delphic responses (χρησμῶν συναγωγή). Vid. *P.W.*
(s.v. Delphoi), 2521. These, however, have perished and we
are now mainly dependent on such fragments of Porphyry's
treatise on oracles (entitled ἐκ λογίων φιλοσοφίας) as Eusebius
incorporated in his refutation of Porphyry's work. Cf. Euseb.
Pr. Ev. iv. 6 : οὗτος (i.e. Porphyry) . . . συναγωγὴν ἐποιήσατο
χρησμῶν τοῦ τε 'Απόλλωνος καὶ τῶν λοιπῶν θεῶν, κ.τ.λ.

[1] This, however, is not peculiar to the Greeks : it is characteristic of all primitive ethics to ignore the act of the will and
concentrate attention upon external acts. Taking cognizance
of the will is the product of advanced civilization and moral
training. Cf. ancient Hebrew ethics.

The Delphic Oracle

The city of Thebes " reeks with incense, rings with prayers for health and cries of woe. The city is sorely vexed and blight is upon her." [1] Why? Because the gods are wroth at the crime of its king. Phoebus bids the people drive out " a defilement of the land." [2] Oedipus declares that he will himself dispel the taint. The action develops. At last poor Oedipus is himself shown to be " the defilement ": he stands self-cursed, self-condemned. He is crushed by the awful discovery that he has committed a twofold crime, parricide and incest. He cries out in agony that he has been " accursed in birth, accursed in wedlock, accursed in the shedding of blood," [3] and in the frenzy of despair blinds himself that he may never again behold the light or look upon such defilement. For the poor victim of fate there is not a word of sympathy : all are convinced that he is indeed " a thing of defilement." He passes his remaining years bereft of crown and sight and happiness. Such is the plot of the great drama, the *Oedipus Tyrannus*, which reveals beyond all others the consequences of this terrible doctrine. The morally-innocent Oedipus is afflicted with the most dreadful penalties at the hands of gods and men.

[1] Soph. O.T. 4 ff.   [2] Ibid. 97.

[3] Ibid. 1184–5, cf. 744–5. Oedipus's outlook, however, is changed in Soph. O.C. There he calmly surveys his action and is convinced of his moral innocence. Cf. O.C. 287: ἥκω γὰρ ἱερὸς εὐσεβής τε καὶ φέρων | ὄνησιν ἀστοῖς τοῖσδ'. Cf. also ibid. 266–73.

134

Influence of the Delphic Oracle on Morality

To the same cause we must attribute the many
legends showing how peoples were scourged by
Heaven for some act of which they were morally
innocent. To such concentration on the mere
physical act we must also attribute the custom at
Athens of arraigning in the Prytaneum before the
four Phylo-Basileis, or Tribe-Kings, an inanimate
object (a stick or a stone, etc.) which had caused
the death of any one without the proved intervention of a human hand : the wood or stone, when
the fact was proved, was actually cast outside the
boundary of the country.[1]

In the course of time, however, as a result no
doubt of the rise and progress of philosophic thought,
this hard ethical system became modified and
account began to be taken at last of the will. The
transition stage is best shown in the famous story
of Orestes.[2] One would imagine it to have been
framed by some clever casuist, who wished to sum
up in one striking example the difficulties which
beset the ancient ethical system. The crime of
Orestes in slaying his mother Clytemnestra has been
prepared by the crimes of anterior generations.
Orestes has been commissioned by the Oracle of
Delphi to avenge the murder of his father, Agamemnon.[3] He is the instrument of divine retribution.
Yet he, too, must be punished. Banished from his

[1] Vid. Grote, "Hist. Gr." iii. p. 294.
[2] Vid. Aesch: Eum.; Eur. Or.
[3] Eur. Or. 29–30 ; Aesch. Eum. 578–80.

The Delphic Oracle

native Argos as a matricide, he is pursued and goaded to madness by the avenging Erinyes. So far the story is quite in accordance with the old-time ethics, the difficulties of which it brings out clearly. Apollo is the heaven-sent avenger of his father's murder : he is bidden by Apollo himself to slay his mother. How, then, with such sanction could he be morally guilty ? Aeschylus feels the difficulty. In his tragedy, the *Eumenides,* he makes Apollo the advocate of Orestes and " cleanser of his murder." [1] As soon as the latter takes his seat as suppliant on the Omphalos, Apollo declares that Orestes' resolution to slay his mother was due to his own bidding. Orestes, therefore, is morally guiltless. There yet remains, however, the social aspect of Orestes' crime. This is set right by the vote of the Areopagus.

Such is the story of Orestes as told by Aeschylus. Euripides, however, goes further. He is not satisfied with the championing of Orestes by Apollo or the vote of acquittal from the Areopagus. He further makes Orestes go to Delphi, where, by way of supplementary expiation, he is bidden to go to Tauric Chersonese and thence fetch the image of Artemis.[2] We have thus reached the second stage of ethical evolution, when the older system is softened and modified by the recognition of the element of free will.

So far there is reference merely to external acts.

[1] Eum. 578–9.   [2] Eur. I.T. 970–8.

Influence of the Delphic Oracle on Morality

We now come to the third stage when there is cognizance of a mere act of the *will*. This is best illustrated by the famous story of Glaucus.[1] Glaucus was a Spartan, who bore the highest character for justice throughout Greece. A certain Milesian came, wishing to entrust his money to him to be kept safely till demanded back. The owner of the money died, and his children came with their tokens to demand their inheritance. Glaucus drove them away, saying that he remembered nothing about such a matter. He went to Delphi, however, and asked the god whether by a false oath he might retain the money. Terrible was the god's response. " Glaucus, son of Epicydes, thus to prevail by an oath to make a booty of the money is an immediate gain. Swear, for death awaits even the man who keepeth his oath. But Oath hath a nameless child, handless and footless. Swift is he to pursue, until, having seized, he destroys the whole race and all the house. But the race of the man who keepeth his oath is more blessed thereafter." Glaucus, hearing these terrible words, was frightened, and entreated the god to pardon him. His repentance was too late. The Pythia declared that " to tempt the god and to do the act were one and the same." [2] This was a truly momentous utterance, a land-

[1] Hdt. vi. 86.

[2] τὸ πειρηθῆναι τοῦ θεοῦ καὶ τὸ ποιῆσαι ἴσον δύνασθαι. Hdt. goes on to say that though Glaucus restored the money he was utterly extirpated from Sparta (ἐκτέτριπταί τε πρόρριζος ἐκ Σπάρτης).

mark in the history of Greek ethics, declaring for
the first time that the essence of sin lay in the
action of the will. It is quite true that it was very
much to the interests of the god to maintain and
proclaim a strict morality in the matter of trusts,[1]
for he was himself the greatest trustee in all Greece,[2]
and he knew how to protect his own [3] not merely
against hostile force but also against theft.[4] Still,
that does not diminish the great ethical value of the
oracle. Again, even if the oracle is not genuine,
still it shows how the idea had been reached at a
comparatively early period. For, Leotychides narrated the story for the edification of the Athenians,
who in the year 487 B.C. were inclined to act like
Glaucus, refusing to restore Aeginetan hostages.[5]
Glaucus, he declared, had lived about three generations before his time.

The same idea of the Oracle's " taking the will
for the deed " is borne out by the fact that the
Pythia is said to have insisted on the value of the
" widow's mite " : the god was said to prefer the
cakes offered from the wallet of the poor man from
Hermione to the oxen with gilded horns in the

[1] Cf. Hdt. i. 159–60 (story of Pactyas) where Apollo of
Branchidae so strongly inculcates the necessity of observing
faithfully the law of not surrendering suppliants to their enemies.

[2] Vid. supr. p. 81, n. 4.

[3] Hdt. viii. 36 ; Paus. x. 23. 1.

[4] Cf. the story of treasure stolen from Delphi and the thief
discovered by means of a wolf (Paus. x. 14. 7).

[5] Vid. Bury, " Hist. Gr." p. 260.

Influence of the Delphic Oracle on Morality

hecatombs of the Thessalian ; the simple cereal gifts of the Arcadian Clearchus to the luxurious presents of the Asiatic Magnesian.[1] Perhaps to this advance to a higher and more humane ethical system we should attribute the lenient treatment of the priestess of Paros and the priest of Heracles Misogynist, already referred to.[2] Certainly the action of the Oracle in these two cases was a marked contrast to the treatment meted out to the erring priestess of Artemis, whom it ordered to be sacrificed to the offended goddess.[3] So, too, we find the Delphic god inculcating mercy in the well-known story of the children of Caphyae in Arcadia, who in play hanged the image of the goddess Artemis. The Caphyaeans stoned the children to death. A plague, however, soon seized upon their women-folk, so that in their distress they had to seek a remedy from Pythian Apollo. The god replied that " they should bury the children, and year by year perform sacrificial rites in their honour, for they had been unjustly slain." [4]

Finally, we have a good illustration of the Oracle's ethical advance, as compared with the ancient system, in a beautiful little story of Aelian.[5] Three

[1] Porphy. De Abst. ii. 16, 17 (quoted by Farnell, op. cit. iv. p. 390).

[2] Vid. supr. p. 116, n. 2.

[3] Vid. Paus. vii. 19. 4 ; supr. p. 129.

[4] Vid. Paus. viii. 23. 6–7. For the Oracle's appeal for mercy for Athens at the end of the Peloponnesian War vid. infr. pp. 165–6.　　　　[5] Var. Hist. iii. 44.

The Delphic Oracle

youths were journeying from the same city to
Delphi to consult the Oracle. Falling in with
robbers, one of the three ran away, while the second,
in trying to defend his companion, accidentally
slew him. To him who had fled the Pythia afterwards replied : " Thou didst not keep nigh to
assist a friend being slain. To thee I shall give
no response. Depart from my most beauteous
sanctuary." [1] But to him who had killed his companion she replied : " Thou didst slay thy friend
in trying to defend him. Thee his blood hath not
defiled ; nay, thou art more clean of hands than
before." [2]

SECTION B : THE DELPHIC MORAL CODE

Taken at its best, what system of moral teaching
does the Oracle of Delphi show ? Its system—if so
it may be called—is meagre, for its moral precepts
are few. It consists in the main of the well-known
maxims inscribed on the temple. And even these
were not due to Apollo, but were aphorisms of
certain philosophers. Being, however, in his temple,
they were naturally ascribed to the inspiration of
Apollo, and must have increased the prestige of the
Oracle in the popular mind.

---

[1] ἀνδρὶ φίλῳ θνήσκοντι παρὼν πέλας οὐκ ἐβοήθεις.
οὔ σε θεμιστεύσω· περικαλλέος ἔξιθι νηοῦ.

[2] ἔκτεινας τὸν ἑταῖρον ἀμύνων· οὔ σ’ ἐμίαινεν
αἷμα, πέλεις δὲ χέρας καθαρώτερος ἢ πάρος ἦσθα.

Influence of the Delphic Oracle on Morality

The history of these sayings—which might be called the Delphic Commandments [1]—is interesting. Pausanias [2] tells us that the Seven Sages of Greece came to Delphi and dedicated to Apollo the famous maxims " Know thyself " (Γνῶθι σεαυτόν) and " Nothing to excess " (Μηδὲν ἄγαν). Plato in the *Protagoras* [3] makes the same statement. Elsewhere [4] Plato mentions a third saying, which was also to be seen in the temple of Delphi, " Go surety, and ruin is at hand " ('Εγγύη· πάρα δ' ἄτη). All three sayings are attributed to Chilon alone by Diodorus [5] and Pliny. [6] As to the number of the maxims inscribed in the temple we are not certain, but these three are the best known. Plutarch [7] says that these three sayings were engraven in the sanctuary by orders of the Amphictyonic Council.

Where in the temple they were dedicated is also uncertain. Pausanias [8] tells us that they were in the fore-temple (ἐν τῷ προνάῳ). According to Diodorus, [9] the three maxims were carved upon a pillar, and Plutarch [10] says that the god by way of salutation addressed each one approaching the temple with the expression " Know thyself." It is probable, then, that the maxims were engraved on one

[1] They are variously called γράμματα, προγράμματα, ῥήματα, παραγγέλματα, γνῶμαι.

[2] x. 24. 1.
[3] p. 343 B.
[4] Charmid. p. 165 B.
[5] Fr. ix. 9. 1.
[6] N. H. vii. 119.
[7] De Garrul. xvii.
[8] x. 24. 1.
[9] Fr. ix. 9. 1.
[10] De E apud Delph. xvii. Cf. Plat. Charm. p. 165.

The Delphic Oracle

of the columns at the entrance of the fore-temple. In the temple, too, were to be seen the mysterious E in wood (supposed to have been dedicated by the Sages) and the golden E dedicated by the Empress Livia.[1]

These maxims were much admired in antiquity. Plutarch[2] speaks of them "as streams pent up within a narrow space. For they have no transparency or lucidity of meaning. But if you examine what has been written and talked about them by such as wish to discover the full meaning of each you will not easily find treatises more lengthy than these." Cicero[3] and Juvenal[4] speak of the divine origin of the maxim "Know thyself." Plato[5] speaks of it as the sum of all knowledge. To Socrates,[6] whose great crusade was directed against sham knowledge, this was the holiest of all texts. He constantly cited it, and strenuously enforced it upon his hearers, interpreting it to mean, Know

[1] Plut. De E apud Delph. iii.

[2] De Pyth. Orac. xxix.: οὐ γὰρ ἔχει τοῦ νοῦ δίοψιν οὐδὲ διαύγειαν, ἀλλ᾽ ἐὰν σκοπῇς τί γέγραπται καὶ λέλεκται περὶ αὐτῶν τοῖς ὅπως ἕκαστον ἔχει βουλομένοις καταμαθεῖν, οὐ ῥᾳδίως τούτων λόγους ἑτέρους εὑρήσεις μακροτέρους. Cf. De E apud Delph. ii.; St. Aug. De Civ. Dei, xviii. 25, ". . . septem appellati sapientes . . . morum nonnulla praecepta sententiarum brevitate complexi sunt."

[3] De Fin. v. § 44, "quod praeceptum quia maius erat quam ut ab homine videretur, idcirco assignatum est deo."

[4] Sat. xi. 27, "e caelo descendit Γνῶθι σεαυτόν."

[5] Charm. p. 166 E.

[6] Vid. Plat. Phaedr. p. 230 A; Charm. p. 166 E; Protag. p. 343 B.

Influence of the Delphic Oracle on Morality

what sort of man thou art and what are thy
capacities in reference to human use. His first
great object was to bring each of his hearers to
take just measure of his own real knowledge or real
ignorance. And for him the recognition of one's
own ignorance was the beginning of wisdom.[1]

Such are the famous moral maxims which were
associated with the Delphic god. What were the
views of the Oracle on other moral questions we
can gather only from certain responses the authenticity of which is unfortunately often doubtful.
Though in its early history the Oracle, as we have
seen, apparently counselled and encouraged human
sacrifice, yet in later times it upheld the sanctity
of human life and the heinousness of the crime of
murder.[2] We remember its answer to the envoy

[1] Cf. Plat. Ap. ix.

[2] Besides the examples cited, vid. also Hdt. vi. 139, for the
penalty imposed by the Delphic Oracle on the Pelasgians of
Lemnos for the murder of Attic women and children, and ibid.
ii. 134, for that imposed on the Delphians who had murdered
Aesop, the fabulist. Again, Apollo was said to have driven
from the temple the slayer of the poet Archilochus (cf. Plin.
N.H. vii. 109). Yet there is one very strange clause in an
inscr. (B.C.H. xvii. p. 384, no. 80). The inscr. is an act of enfranchisement, dating apparently fairly late. Dioclea, a female
slave, is manumitted, but, as sometimes happens, she has to
remain with her master for some time. If a child is born to her
during this period she is given permission by the Oracle to put
it to death, if she pleases (εἰ δέ τι γένοιτο ἐκ Διοκλέας | τέκνον
ἐν τῷ τᾶς παραμονᾶς χρόνωι, εἴ κα μὲν θέληι ἀποπνεῖξαι Διοκλέα,
ἐξουσίαν ἐχέτω). There seems no reason to doubt the reading
ἀποπνεῖξαι (lit. " throttle "). This treatment which the Oracle
sanctions cannot be attributed to the fact that the child is

The Delphic Oracle

of Procles, the blood-stained tyrant of Epidaurus.[1] We have also the Oracle's terrible denunciation of the murderers from Sybaris.[2] " Go from my tripod," said Apollo. " Much dripping blood yet clinging to thy hands shuts thee out from the threshold of stone. To thee I shall give no response. Having slain at the altar of Hera the servant of the Muses, thou hast not escaped the vengeance of Heaven. For evil-doers the issue of justice must not be delayed. To them must no pardon be given, even were they children of Zeus." So sacred was human life for the Oracle, that according to Antiphon the accidental shedding of even a slave's blood was regarded by it as producing a stain.[3]

The Oracle championed the sacred cause of truth. Again and again Apollo asserted his own veracity, and, indeed, was regarded as the god of truth.[4] " He is the god that most loves truth," [5] said Plutarch. The chorus of youths in Plato's ideal state swear to the truth of their words in the

the offspring of a slave, for it is expressly stated that the child, if reared, will be free (εἰ δὲ θέλοι τρέφειν, ἔστω τὸ τρεφόμενον ἐλεύθερον). However, child-life was not so sacred in antiquity as now. Cf. the Spartan custom of exposing rejected children to die on Mt. Taygetus (vid. Plut. Lyc. xvi.).

[1] Vid. supr. p. 94.

[2] Ael. Var. Hist. iii. 43 : βαῖν' ἀπ' ἐμῶν τριπόδων· ἔτι τοι φόνος ἀμφὶ χέρεσσι | πουλὺς ἀποστάζων ἀπὸ λαΐνου οὐδοῦ ἐρύκει, κ.τ.λ. (With the expression φόνος ἀμφὶ χέρεσσι cf. Shakespeare, " Macbeth," v. ii. " His secret murders sticking to his hands.")

[3] p. 764.   [4] Vid. supr. p. 62.   [5] De E ap. Delph. vi.

name of the god of truth, Paean-Apollo.[1]   Truth
was the foster-nurse of Apollo.[2]   The Pythian god
came to be regarded as the umpire of the Greek
intellectual world, whose great aim was the search
after truth.   The Delphic Oracle, as we have seen,
showed at all times consideration and respect for
philosophers.[3]   The best example is, of course, the
famous response regarding Socrates.   Chaerephon
in his enthusiastic admiration for his master asked
the Pythia whether any one was wiser than Socrates.
The answer was that there was none.[4]   This proved
a turning-point in the life of the great philosopher.[5]
In consequence of it he at once set about testing
the truth of the Oracle—not but that he believed
in Apollo's prophetic powers, for he thought it
necessary to set the highest value upon the statement of the god.[6]   As a result of his inquiry in the
case of poets, politicians and craftsmen he came to

[1] Legg. 664 C.

[2] Vid. Farnell, op. cit. iv. p. 242.

[3] Vid. supr. pp. 75–6.

[4] Plat. Ap. v.: ἤρετο γὰρ δὴ εἴ τις ἐμοῦ εἴη σοφώτερος. ἀνεῖλεν
οὖν ἡ Πυθία μηδένα σοφώτερον εἶναι.   Cf. Paus. i. 22. 8, who says
that the Pythia bore witness that Socrates was the wisest of men
—a title which she refused to give to Anacharsis, though he
came to Delphi to obtain it.   The exact response given to
Chaerephon was : σοφὸς Σοφοκλῆς, σοφώτερος δ' Εὐριπίδης, | ἀνδρῶν
δὲ πάντων Σωκράτης σοφώτατος.   Note the Iambic form of this
χρησμός, showing its late origin.   Vid. supr. p. 68, n. 3, and
App. B for the form in which the responses were given.

[5] Vid. Burnet, " Gr. Philos." pt. i. pp. 135–6.

[6] Plat. Ap. vii. ; cf. Socrates' bidding Xenophon consult
the Delphic Oracle, vid. Xen. Anab. iii. 1, 5.

the conclusion that the god was right. For, he was wiser, he thought, than other men, who had a repute for wisdom, at least in this, that he was aware of his own ignorance, whereas they were not. Henceforth he regarded himself as having a mission to his fellow-citizens—a mission imposed upon him by the god,[1] a mission to prove to men the worthlessness of all human wisdom, and that the god alone was wise.[2] Thus did the Oracle confer a lasting service upon Greece in the domain of moral thought. For, the movement which Socrates initiated did not die with him, but lived on and flourished in his disciples, who doubtless were all, like Plato, its enthusiastic propagators.

The Oracle inculcated a lofty morality in the case of oaths and of trust.[3] It condemned theft ;[4] indeed, the god inspired a superstitious dread of stealing from his sanctuary, for he was regarded as an adept at discovering treasures stolen from his temple.[5] It rebuked Spartan avarice,[6] and con-

[1] Ap. xviii.   [2] Ibid. ix.

[3] Cf. the case of Glaucus, Hdt. vi. 86. Vid. supr. pp. 137–8.

[4] Cf. Plat. Legg. p. 914 B, who says that the god of Delphi is the best judge in the matter of considerable embezzlements.

[5] Cf. the story in Paus. (x. 14. 7) of a thief who had stolen from the god's treasures and was discovered by the howling of a wolf. Men found guilty of stealing from the Delphic treasures were summarily dealt with by being hurled from the rock Hyampea. Vid. Ael. Var. Hist. x. 5.

[6] Cf. ἁ φιλοχρηματία Σπάρταν ὀλεῖ, ἄλλο δὲ οὐδέν, quoted as a Delphic response by Farnell (op. cit. iv. p. 216, n.) from Aristotle.

demned Sybarite luxury.[1] The Pythian god commended honest poverty, for he declared the poor old man of Arcadia to be happier on his little farm and frugal fare than Gyges with his kingdom and his wealth.[2]

In the matter of morality in the restricted sense, however, the standard of the Oracle does not seem to have been in any way in advance of its time. It is true, of course, that it insisted on the Pythia's living a virtuous life.[3] Yet we seek in vain for any condemnation or disapproval of the moral corruption which was so prevalent in Greece even in the hey-day of its glory. Nay, we have some positive evidence of its approval of such. For, did it not accept the offerings of Rhodopis [4] and Phryne,[5] giving the latter's image a place " among captains and kings " [6]—aye, though the offerings of both were but tithes from the " wages of sin " ? We must, however, judge the action of the Oracle in this matter, not according to the lofty standard of the Gospel, but according to the standard of pagan antiquity, which was emphatically not high, and which could regard the conduct of a Rhodopis or a Phryne as " the smallest of Greek faults." [7]

---

[1] Diod. xii. 10. 5.
[2] Vid. Plin. N.H. vii. 151.
[3] Vid. supr. p. 52.
[4] Hdt. ii. 135 ; Plut. De Pyth. Orac. xiv
[5] Paus. x. 15. 1 ; Plut. De Pyth. Orac. xiv.
[6] Plut. ibid.
[7] Plut. De Pyth. Orac. xv.

The Delphic Oracle

SECTION C : DELPHIC ESCHATOLOGY

What was the nature of the Delphic eschatology ?
The early Greek recked but little of the life to come.
For him death meant the " end all " of human joys
and sorrows. He had no doctrines of rewards or
punishments in the future life. The lot of all was
the same : all alike went down to the house of
Hades, there to pass a shadowy, unreal existence.[1]
But apparently as a result of its association with
the cult of Dionysus, the Apolline religion came
to include two very important doctrines—that of
the immortality of the soul and the existence of a
life of happiness beyond the tomb. Conspicuous
virtue could raise a mortal to a share in divine
honours [2]—aye, could make him a ruler in the
realm of spirits.[3] Chastisements and recompenses
of the future life entered into Delphic theology.
We may feel sure that Pindar, whom the Oracle
bade have an equal share of first-fruits with Apollo
himself,[4] was but voicing its sentiments when, with

[1] But vid. Hom. Od. iv. 561–4, where it is declared to
Menelaus that he is " not destined to meet his doom in Argos,
but that the immortals will convey him to the Elysian plain,
but the world's end, where is fair-haired Rhadamanthys, where
life is easiest for men."

[2] Cf. hero-worship.

[3] Cf. Rhadamanthys " who is in bliss " ($\epsilon\hat{\upsilon}$ $\pi\acute{\epsilon}\pi\rho\alpha\gamma\epsilon\nu$) because of his " blameless thoughts," Pind. P. ii. 73–4,
and " shareth for ever the judgment-seat of the Father," O.
ii. 76.

[4] Vid. supr. p. 77.

148

almost Scriptural clearness, he contrasts the future
life of the virtuous and the wicked. " The good,
having the sun shining for ever more . . . share
among the honoured gods a life that knoweth no
tears . . . where around the Isles of the Blest the
ocean-breezes blow, and there is a blaze of golden
flowers." [1] But " the lawless spirits, whose sins
committed in this realm of Zeus are judged by one
that passeth sentence stern and inevitable," are
punished immediately after death.[2] The cult of
heroes, so strongly encouraged by Delphi, indicated
what was the lot of the just ; fear of future torments
was inculcated by sensible images. In the Lesche
of the Cnidians at Delphi was to be found the
famous painting by Polygnotus, whose scenes were
all borrowed from the infernal world.[3]

Section D : The Apolline Doctrine of Katharsis or Purification

Of great importance in the Delphic moral system
is the doctrine of katharsis or purification. " To
Apollo catharsios suppliants addressed themselves
to be freed from every stain . . . no one must approach his temple who has not been purified by
water or by sacrifices. . . . He is implored against
maladies, and especially against epidemics, by those

---

[1] O. ii. 61–80. Cf. Matt. xxv. ; Apoc. iv. vii.

[2] O. ii. 57–60.

[3] Vid. Paus. x. 28–31, and Frazer's " Comm." Cf. Myers,
" Essays," p. 50 ff.

The Delphic Oracle

who have first performed lustrations."[1] In the case
of the shedding of blood, even where the homicide
was justifiable (φόνος δίκαιος) purification seems to
have been always necessary.[2] Apollo himself had
set the example of this. For, after having right-
eously slain the Python of Parnassus, he had to flee
to the vale of Tempe, there to be purified by the
cleansing laurel.[3]

Let us cite a few examples of this function of
Apollo as Καθάρσιος.[4] Achilles is purified in Lesbos
by Apollo, Artemis and Leto of the blood of Ther-

[1] " C'est à lui que s'adressaient les suppliants pour être délivrés
de toute souillure. . . . Personne ne doit s'approcher de son
temple, s'il ne s'est auparavant purifié par l'eau ou par les
sacrifices. . . . On l'implore contre les maladies et surtout
contre les épidémies après avoir fait des lustrations " (Darem-
berg et Saglio, "Dict. des Ant." s.v. Apollon).

[2] Cf. Plat. Legg. 865 C: εἴ τις ἄκων ἀπέκτεινέ τινα φίλιον. . .
καθαρθεὶς κατὰ τὸν ἐκ Δελφῶν κομισθέντα περὶ τούτων νόμον, ἔστω
καθαρός. (For an exact parallel in Hebrew legislation vid. Lev.
iv. 29, where it is laid down that a " sin-offering " must be made
in atonement for sinning unwittingly, which, too, causes a stain.)
Cf. P.W. (s.v. Apollon, 24); Bouché-Leclercq, op. cit. iii. p. 180.

[3] Vid. Ael. Var. Hist. iii. 1: ἐνταῦθά τοί φασι παῖδες Θετταλῶν
καὶ τὸν Ἀπόλλωνα τὸν Πύθιον καθήρασθαι . . . τῆς Γῆς ἔτι ἐχούσης
τὸ μαντεῖον. Acc. to Hypoth. Pind. P. (quoted by Mommsen,
"Delph." p. 294, n. 3), Apollo, having been purified in Crete at
the house of Chrysothemis, thence came to Thessalian Tempe,
whence he brought the laurel. According to another legend,
Ap. was purified by the Cretan Carmanor (Paus. x. 7. 2; ii. 7. 7).
According to yet another legend, Ap. was purified from the
blood of the Cyclopes, by going into servitude with Admetus
(vid. Eur. Alc. 3–8).

[4] For Apollo Καθάρσιος vid. Aesch. Eum. 63; cf. P.W. (s.v.
Apollon, 15).

Influence of the Delphic Oracle on Morality

sites.[1] Orestes [2] and Theseus [3] are purified at Troezen by Apollo, the former from the blood of his mother, Clytemnestra, the latter from the blood of the Pallantidae. Bacis at the bidding of Apollo purifies from madness the Lacedaemonian women.[4] The most famous instance quoted from historical times is that of the purification of Athens. The Athenians, visited by a plague in consequence of the affair of Cylon, consulted the Delphic Oracle as to a means of deliverance. The god commanded them to get their city purified, and accordingly they summoned the Cretan Epimenides, who in 596 B.C. performed the desired task by certain mysterious rites and sacrifices.[5]

Whence did Apollo derive his title of Καθάρσιος ? Whence came his power of cleansing from every stain of sin ? Plato has reduced to four the offices of Apollo—musician, prophet, physician, archer.[6] We find two of these offices—those of physician and prophet—felicitously combined in the epithet

[1] Epic of Arctinus (quoted by Farnell, op. cit. ii. p. 597).

[2] Paus. ii. 31. 8.   [3] Paus. i. 22. 2.

[4] Schol. Ar. Pax (quoted by Farnell, op. cit. iv. p. 411).

[5] Vid. Plut. Solon, xii. ; Diog. Laert. i. x. 3 : . . . ἔχρησεν ἡ Πυθία καθῆραι τὴν πόλιν· οἱ δὲ πέμπουσι ναῦν τε καὶ Νικίαν τὸν Νικηράτου εἰς Κρήτην, καλοῦντες τὸν Ἐπιμενίδην.

[6] Craty. p. 405 B: (δύναμιν) μουσικήν τε καὶ μαντικὴν καὶ ἰατρικὴν καὶ τοξικήν. Cf. Menander the rhetor (quoted by Bouché-Leclercq, op. cit. iii. p. 6): δυνάμεις τοῦ θεοῦ· τοξική, μαντική, ἰατρική, μουσική. Cf. Hor. Carm. Saec. 61-4, " augur et fulgente decorus arcu | Phoebus acceptusque novem Camenis | qui salutari levat arte fessos | corporis artus."

The Delphic Oracle

applied to him by Aeschylus when he calls him
" physician-seer " ('Ιατρόμαντις).[1]   The association
of the two offices was natural.   In Homeric times
it is Apollo who sends pestilence,[2] then by a natural
sequence he is also the god who removes it.[3]   To
him the Paean—the joyous song of deliverance from
the scourge of plague—is sung.[4]   He is invoked to
find a remedy for woes.[5]   He is the Great Physician
('Ιατρός) who is invoked to heal.   But all this healing
power arose from his mantic power : he is 'Ιατρός
because he is Μάντις.   For among ancient peoples
—as indeed is the case among all primitive society—
medicine was regarded as a divine revelation.   If,
then, Apollo is " physician-seer," who can heal all
bodily ills, what is more natural than to regard
him also as the cleanser of all moral disease and
defilement ?   And although Apollo had not the
monopoly of the cathartic power—for Zeus Meilichios,[6] Demeter,[7] and above all Dionysus,[8] pos-

---

[1] Eum. 62: ἰατρόμαντις δ' ἐστι καὶ τερασκόπος.   Greek mythology represented Asclepius—" the blameless physician " who
became the god of medicine—as the son of Apollo and Coronis
(cf. Paus. ii. 26. 6 ; Ov. Met. II. 628–9) or Arsinoe (cf. Cic.
De Nat. Deor. iii. 22, 57).

[2] Vid. Il. i. 42 ff. ;   Paus. ix. 36. 3.

[3] Cf. epithets 'Αλεξίκακος (Paus. i. 3. 4), Παίων (= Παιήων,
Παιώνιος) (Paus. i. 34. 2), 'Ακέσιος (Paus. vi. 24. 5), 'Επικούριος
(Paus. viii. 41. 5).

[4] Cf. Schol. Ar. Plut. 636.

[5] Eur. Alc. 220 ff.   [6] Paus. ii. 20. 1.

[7] Cf. the Eleusinian Mysteries, vid. Farnell, op. cit. iv.
pp. 162, 168.

[8] Vid. Farnell, op. cit. v. p. 212.

Influence of the Delphic Oracle on Morality

sessed it too—yet, because he was the purest [1] and the brightest of all the bright Olympians, and because Delphi had already obtained religious hegemony at an early age, it was natural that men should look to Apollo for a remedy.

When and whence this doctrine and ritual of purification were introduced into the Apolline religion we cannot say for certain. It is true that of katharsis in Homer there is little or none. In the *Iliad* " the son of Atreus bids the folk purify themselves. They purified themselves and cast the defilements into the sea and did sacrifice unto Apollo " ; [2] and in the *Odyssey* we are told how Telemachus " went far apart to the shore of the sea, laved his hands in the grey sea and prayed unto Athene." [3] In the *Iliad* [4] and *Odyssey* [5] we have instances of the use of holy water preparatory to the offering of sacrifice. The words of Hector, when he declares that he shrinks " from pouring out with hands unwashed the shining wine unto Zeus," and asserts that it is " unlawful for one stained with mud and gore to make prayer unto the cloud-enwrapped

---

[1] Cf. the epithet Φοῖβος, which refers probably not to " light " but to the *purity* of the god, who shunned all defilement. Vid. Plut. De E apud Delph. xx : Φοῖβον δὲ δήπου τὸ καθαρὸν καὶ ἀγνὸν οἱ παλαιοὶ πᾶν ὠνόμαζον, ὡς ἔτι Θεσσαλοὶ τοὺς ἱερέας ἐν ταῖς ἀποφράσιν ἡμέραις αὐτοὺς ἐφ᾽ ἑαυτῶν ἔξω διατρίβοντας, οἶμαι, φοιβονομεῖσθαι λέγουσι. Cf. Eur. Alc. 22.

[2] i. 312–4. The expression means that they bathed in the sea " which washes away all the evils of men " (θάλασσα κλύζει πάντα τἀνθρώπων κακά, Eur. I.T. 1193).

[3] ii. 260–1.   [4] i. 449.   [5] iii. 445.

153

son of Kronos,"[1] seem to contain a trace of the idea—otherwise ignored in Homer—that homicide involves personal stain requiring purification.

Such are the meagre references in Homer to the cathartic doctrine and ritual. Some writers are inclined to argue from this well-nigh complete silence of the Homeric poems on the question of purification that the poet must have been ignorant of it. Dr. Farnell, who is certainly a great authority on such matters, holds it as reasonable to maintain the " somewhat late origin " of cathartic ceremonies in Apolline ritual, adducing as proofs, first, the fact that the association of the story of Orestes with Apollo is post-Homeric ; secondly, that no such ceremonies were connected with the earliest Apolline festivals, e.g. those of the Carnea or Hyacinthia.; thirdly, that Homer is silent on the question of regarding homicide as a personal stain. Yet he admits that it is " difficult to believe that the whole ritual of purification and the conception of miasma . . . were developed in Greece wholly in the post-Homeric age."[2]

Nevertheless, it seems to be probable enough that what is generally regarded as the introduction is really but the *revival* of the cathartic element. For, in the first place, it would be strange indeed if such ritual, which is so prevalent in all primitive society, should have been unknown to the pre-Homeric Greek. Again, the purification

[1] Il. vi. 266-8.   [2] Farnell, op. cit. iv. p. 298.

rites connected with the Stepterion—which feast we shall presently discuss—where the boy-priest representing Apollo goes to be purified in the vale of Tempe—point to an ancient prehistoric sanctuary in the distant North, with which purification was strongly associated. As to Dr. Farnell's arguments, it is noticeable that all three arguments are *ex silentio*. But the argument "from silence" is usually weak, and certainly in this connexion, in the case of Homer, it is unusually so. The ignoring of cathartic ritual by Homer may well have been due to his general tendency to depreciate everything aboriginal. What scant notice he takes of the old chthonian divinities! So, too, we may argue, he takes but scant notice of the ritual which was specially associated with the cults of the chthonian and nature divinities. Homer is all for Zeus and the Olympian religion, and consequently he ignores the whole doctrine and ritual of katharsis because of its special association with the religion which the Greeks came to supplant. It is even possible that the Greeks for the more effective suppression of the older ritual of the conquered race would have temporarily suppressed similar elements in their own. The silence of Homer on the subject of katharsis would on this hypothesis be easy to understand.

The revival of the cathartic ritual in later times would be due perhaps partly to the association at Delphi of Apollo with Dionysus, in whose worship

The Delphic Oracle

the doctrine and practice of purification played so important a rôle,[1] partly to the influence of Crete, where from the oldest times a cathartic ritual seems to have been attached to the cult of Cretan Zeus.[2] That it was fittingly associated with the Apolline worship we have already seen.[3] As to the argument that the association of the purification of Orestes with Apollo is post-Homeric, we may answer that this is not at all surprising owing to the general silence of Homer on such matters. Finally, the argument from the absence of purification ritual in the worship of Apollo Κάρνειος and 'Υακίνθιος,[4] may be answered by saying that the Carnea and Hyacinthia date from a period preceding the revival of katharsis in the Apolline worship.

As regards the means of purification (καθαρμοί), a distinctive feature of the Apolline ritual was the

[1] Vid. Farnell, op. cit. iv. p. 300.

[2] Ibid. i. pp. 37–8; iv. p. 300.   [3] Vid. supr. pp. 151–2.

[4] 'Υάκινθος is probably a pre-Hellenic vegetation-divinity of the Peloponnesus, who was supplanted by Apollo. The first part of the word seems to contain the same √ as Skt. *Yuvaçás*, Lat. *iuvencus*, Goth. *juggs*, Germ. *jung*, Eng. *young*, Ir. óɢ. Hence the god was represented in legend as a youth. The second part of the word contains the " nth " termination, which, according to R. S. Conway, is Eteo-Cretan (apparently belonging to the " Aryan " family of languages, cf. Corinth, apparently from √ of κείρω, " cut," referring to the Isthmus). This termination is found in a fair number of place-names throughout Greece : cf. Corinth, Zacynthus, Cernithus. This would seem to show that the Eteo-Cretans, " the genuine Cretans " (Hom. Od. xix. 176), before the coming of Apollo dominated the whole Aegean area. Vid. R. M. Burrows, " Cretan Discoveries," p. 153. Ridgeway (op. cit. I. p. 202) identifies the Eteo-Cretans with the Pelasgians.

Influence of the Delphic Oracle on Morality

use of the laurel, the sacred tree which was so closely associated with the god. Water naturally had a cleansing effect in the Apolline as well as in other ritual : holy water (χέρνιψ) was not unfrequently placed outside temples and houses for the use of those who entered.[1] This lustral water was probably sprinkled by means of a laurel branch [2] on the person labouring under defilement (ἐναγής).

Another element of lustration in the Apolline katharsis was washing with the blood of a pig, which was specially used in purification from homicide.[3] The reason why pig's blood was thus used was because the pig was pre-eminently sacred to the chthonian powers.[4] By the act of homicide the slayer had offended the Earth and the ghost : " the blood drunk by the Earth " [5] clamoured for punishment on its shedder.[6] Hence, washing with pig's blood was naturally the means for reconciling the guilty one with the nether powers.

The crowning rite of the Apolline katharsis was the " Stepterion." [7] Our chief authorities on the

---

[1] For the use of holy water (χέρνιψ) and lustrations therewith (χέρνιβες, Lat: *malluviae*) vid. Lys. 108. 1 ; Dem. Lept. 505 ; Thuc. iv. 97 ; Eur. Or. 1602, Phoen. 662, Alc. 100.

[2] Cf. Clem. Alex. Strom. p. 674 (quoted by Farnell, op. cit. iv. p. 429) : ὁ μὲν γὰρ ἐπιρραίνων τὸ πλῆθος δάφνης κλάδοις. . . . Cf. Ps. li. 7, " thou shalt sprinkle me with hyssop, and I shall be cleansed."

[3] Vid. Farnell, op. cit. iv. pp. 303–4.

[4] Ibid. iv. p. 303 ; iii. p. 220.

[5] Aesch. Cho. 66: αἵματ' ἐκποθένθ' ὑπὸ χθονός.

[6] Cf. Gen. iv. 10, " the voice of thy brother's blood crieth to me from the earth."

[7] The form Σεπτήριον (as if from σέβω, " worship ") is now

157

The Delphic Oracle

question are Plutarch [1] and Aelian. [2] Combining the accounts given by both writers we form some such picture as this of the ceremony. The Stepterion was one of the three Enneaterides [3] (i.e. festivals held every nine years) at Delphi, and seemed to be an imitation of the combat of the god against the Python and his flight to Tempe. On a certain day (probably early in summer) a noble Delphian boy, both of whose parents were alive (ἀμφιθαλής), accompanied by a band of Delphian youths chosen from the best families, was escorted by certain sacred women called the " Oleae " [4] carrying torches. They proceeded in silence to a cabin that was constructed near the Pythian temple in the form of a royal palace, which was regarded as the dwelling-place of the Python. [5]

discarded for the better supported Στεπτήριον, which is best derived from στέφω, the reference being to the purificatory laurel-crowns brought by the procession from Tempe.

[1] De Def. Orac. xv.

[2] Var. Hist. iii. 1.

[3] Plut. Quaest. Graec. xii. The other two were Ἡρωΐς and Χαρίλα, both being women's festivals.

[4] Plut. De Def. Orac. xv. αἱ Ὀλεῖαι seems to be the true reading here for the Ms. μὴ αἰόλα. For those women figuring in the Dionysiac festival, Agrionia, at Orchomenus in Boeotia, vid. Plut. Quaest. Graec. xxxviii.; cf. Smith, " Dict. of Ant." s.v. Agrionia ; vid. supr. p. 128.

[5] A large open space was found by the French excavators in front of the portico of the Athenians. It is of circular form, surrounded with seats. Most probably it is the ἅλως of Plutarch (De Def. Orac. xv.), where the slaughter of the dragon by Apollo was represented at the Stepterion. Vid. *B.C.H.* xvii. p. 569.

Influence of the Delphic Oracle on Morality

This they set fire to, and without looking round fled through the doors of the temple. Then came the " wanderings up and down, and the servitude of the boy, and the rites of purification at Tempe " : the boy-leader feigned to go into exile and even servitude. They proceeded to Tempe, where they were purified [2] at an altar, and offered a magnificent sacrifice. Then, having plucked the laurel-branches, they wove for themselves garlands and returned along the Sacred Pythian Way. At a village near Larissa, called " Deipnias " (" the place of the meal," δεῖπνον), the boy-leader took a solemn meal.[3] Thence the procession came in triumph to Delphi. The sacred laurel they brought back was used for weaving chaplets with which the victors in the Pythian games were crowned.

Such was the great rite of the Stepterion. It is clear that in the main it was merely expiatory. There is, however, one difficulty in the story. It is said that " a cabin in imitation of a royal palace " was constructed to represent the dwelling of the Python.[4] But why should the dwelling of the Python be represented as a royal palace ? We have no myth or legend to the effect that the Python lived in any such residence. Dr. Farnell

[1] Plut. De Def. Orac. xv.

[2] ἁγνισθεὶς ἔνι Τέμπεσσιν, Paean of Ariston. l. 17 (*B.C.H.* xvii. p. 561).

[3] Steph. Byz. s.v. Δειπνιάς (quoted by Farnell, op. cit. iv. p. 426).

[4] Plut. De Def. Orac. xv.

The Delphic Oracle

does not touch the question. Miss Harrison [1] would explain it by saying that the Python represents the "Year-Daimon" regarded as a king and reigning nine years—like Minos—and envisaged by a snake. She compares Cecrops and Cenchreus, who were snakes. But, in the first place, what proof is there that the "Year-Daimon" was represented as a king? Again, does the Python represent the "Year-Daimon"? Surely he represents Earth? I should venture to give the following explanation. The hut originally represented, not the palace of a snake (what has a snake to do with a palace?), but the tent in which Apollo received a preliminary purification. We may compare the tent in which Orestes was purified at Troezen.[2] The tent being thus contaminated, was burned.[3] The boy-leader and his band fled "without looking back" (ἀνεπιστρεπτεί) [4] to escape the evil influences which might be about. But he who was originally purified was the "King Apollo." Hence the tent should be like a royal palace. In course of time, however, it came to be transformed in the popular mind into the dwelling of the Python.

[1] "Themis," p. 428.

[2] Paus. ii. 31. 11.

[3] For the burning of unclean things cf. Lev. xiii. With the ritual of burning the Python's cabin at Delphi Frazer ("Comm. Paus." v. p. 55) quotes a very interesting parallel from savage myth. In Dahomey the man who slays a "fetish-snake" enters a hut, which is set on fire. He escapes as best he can from the tribesmen who pursue him till he reaches a river.

[4] Plut. De Def. Orac. xv.

Influence of the Delphic Oracle on Morality

But what was the relation of the Stepterion to the Python? It is probable that originally it had nothing to do with the slaying of the Python by Apollo, as is shown by the Boeotian Daphnephoria.[1] This latter feast had no connexion whatever with the Python-legend. At Thebes every nine years a procession (headed as at Delphi by a youth, both of whose parents were alive, elected for the year as priest of Ismenian Apollo) used to bear laurel-branches—hence the name—to the temple of Apollo. It is quite reasonable, then, to maintain that this procession of laurel-bearers along the Sacred Way to Delphi was part of a great public lustration ceremony connecting Delphi with a great shrine of Apollo in the North. Afterwards, however, this expiatory rite became mixed up with the Python-legend. The idea arose that the pure nature of Apollo was stained by the blood of the Python. Then it was thought that all the purification in Tempe and the laurel-bearing to Delphi were but a commemoration of what Apollo himself had once done.

What was the moral value of purification in the Apolline religion? Here, too, we find an ethical growth. In Homer there is no idea that the shedding of blood involved a personal stain, though, as we have seen, there is trace of the idea in the state-

[1] Vid. Paus. ix. 10. 4 ; Proclus, Chrestomath. c. 11 (quoted by Farnell, op. cit. iv. p. 427). Vid. Smith's " Dict. of Ant." s.v. Daphnephoria, I. p. 597.

The Delphic Oracle

ment of Hector, already quoted.[1] In the age following Homer, however, we find the idea strongly
developed that the shedding of blood in every case
involved a defilement (ἄγος), which only elaborate
ceremonies of lustration could wipe out. But the
stain was *physical* rather than moral. " The secret
murders sticking to the hands " were a reality. Hence
the punishment inflicted upon the shedding of blood,
even when, as in the case of Oedipus, the shedder
was morally innocent. Hence, too, the idea that the
stain could be wiped out by mere external washing.

Early purification, then, was purely ceremonial,
having no reference whatever to cleanliness of soul.
In later times, however, just as the Oracle rose to
a recognition of the importance of the will in human
acts, so too, if we are to take as authentic two
very beautiful χρησμοί in the Anthology, it rose
to a more lofty conception of purification, deeming
true purification to consist in cleanliness of soul.
" Stranger," said the Pythia, " if pure of soul, enter
into the sanctuary of the god of purity, having but
touched the sacred stream. For lustration is an
easy matter for the good. As for the wicked man,
not the whole ocean with its waves could wash him
clean." [2] The second brings out with Scriptural

[1] Vid. supr. p. 153.
[2] Anth. Pal. 14, 71 :

Ἀγνὸς εἰς τέμενος καθαροῦ, ξένε, δαίμονος ἔρχου
ψυχὴν νυμφαίου νάματος ἀψάμενος·
ὡς ἀγαθοῖς κεῖται βαιὴ λιβάς . ἄνδρα δὲ φαῦλον
οὐδ' ἂν ὁ πᾶς νίψαι νάμασιν Ὠκεανός.

Cf. Cic. Laws, ii. 10, "animi tabes nec diuturnitate evanescere

162

Influence of the Delphic Oracle on Morality

clearness the futility of mere external purification—
the mere Pharisaical cleansing of the outside of the
cup. "The temples of the gods are thrown open
to all good men, nor is there any need of purification. No defilement can ever touch virtue. But
whoso is baneful of heart, withdraw ; for the
washing of thy body will never cleanse thy soul." [1]
With this important question of the Apolline katharsis we bring the discussion of the moral influence
of Delphi to a close.

nec amnibus ullis elui potest " ; Shak. " Macb." ii. 2, 60, " will
all great Neptune's ocean wash this blood clean from my
hand ? "

[1] Anth. Pal. no. 74:

'Ἱρὰ θεῶν ἀγαθοῖς ἀναπέπταται, οὐδὲ καθαρμῶν
χρειώ· τῆς ἀρετῆς ἥψατο οὐδὲν ἄγος.
ὅστις δ' οὐλοὸς ἦτορ, ἀπόστιχε. οὔποτε γὰρ σὴν
ψυχὴν ἐκνίψει σῶμα διαινόμενον.

Indeed the same idea of the necessity of purity of conscience is
borne out by the oracle directed against the murderers from
Sybaris. Vid. supr. p. 144. Cf. Lucan, Phars. v. 139 : " Paean
solitus templis arcere nocentes " ; Philostr. Apollon. of Tyana,
iii. 42 : ἡ τέχνη τοὺς ἐς θεοῦ φοιτῶντας ἐπί τῷ χρήσασθαι καθαροὺς
κελεύει βαδίζοντας φοιτᾶν, ἢ " ἔξιθι τοῦ νεώ " πρὸς αὐτοὺς ἐρεῖ. Apparently the Eleusinian Mysteries required also that the initiated
be " pure in hand and soul." Cf. Liban. Or. Corinth. vol. iv.
p. 356 (Reiske), quoted by Farnell, op. cit. v. p. 365. Cf. also
Ar. Ran. 355 : ὅστις . . . γνώμῃ μὴ καθαρεύει.

CHAPTER VI

THE DECLINE AND FALL OF THE DELPHIC ORACLE

Section A : Transition Stages in the Delphic Influence

THE sixth century B.C. shows the Delphic Oracle at the height of its power. It begins with the First Sacred War (circ. 590 B.C.), in which the Amphictyons, the crusaders of antiquity, warmly espoused the cause of the god, and delivered his shrine from the tyranny and exactions of the Crisaeans.[1] In the middle of this century, Croesus sent those gifts which in the days of Herodotus were the wonder and the glory of the sanctuary.[2] In 548 B.C. the temple was burnt to the ground,[3] but from its ashes rose another of far greater magnificence, reared by the princely Alcmaeonidae.[4] The closing act of this period, the zenith of the power of the Oracle, was one of supreme importance for Greece—the liberation of Athens from the tyranny of Hippias.[5]

The Persian wars, however, show, though almost

---

[1] For the First Sacred War vid. Paus. x. 37. 6 ; cf. Bury, " Hist. Gr." pp. 157–9.

[2] Vid. Herod. i. 50–1, supr. p. 70.

[3] Vid. supr. p. 85.   [4] Ibid.   [5] Hdt. v. 63.

Decline and Fall of the Delphic Oracle

imperceptibly, a turn in the tide of the greatness of the Oracle. In the severest ordeal which Greece had yet to face, when her national life was threatened with extinction, the Delphic god, as we have seen,[1] had nothing to offer but "counsels of cowardice" tantamount to submission. And though, when the danger was past, the Greeks presented first-fruits to Apollo, it cannot have escaped them, when the flush of victory was over, that they had triumphed without his aid.

The second stage in the downward course is marked by the Peloponnesian War (431–404 B.C.), when, for the first time in its history, the Oracle showed open and gross partiality. Not only did it predict success for the Lacedaemonians, but it declared its determination to side with them whether invited or not.[2] It must, however, be conceded that it was not wholly unreasonable or unjust for the Oracle to side with Sparta, but yet even for prudential considerations it should have maintained at least a show of impartiality. The Oracle acted up to its promise : Delphi became a post for Lacedaemonian troops.[3] Aelian,[4] indeed, tells us that at the close of the long struggle, when the Athenian power was crushed, and Athens lay beneath the heel of the conqueror, the Delphic god

[1] pp. 87–8 (supr.).   [2] Thuc. i. 118, 123.   [3] Thuc. iii. 101.
[4] Var. Hist. iv. 6: . . . ἡνίκα ἐβούλοντο Λακεδαιμόνιοι τὴν Ἀθηναίων ἀφανίσαι πόλιν, ἠρώτησαν τὸν θεὸν καὶ ἀπεκρίνατο τὴν κοινὴν ἑστίαν Ἑλλάδος μὴ κινεῖν.

pleaded for mercy for the fallen foe. This we would gladly believe, but unfortunately the story lacks firm foundation.

The third stage in the definite decline of the Oracle we reach in the Second Sacred War (357–46 B.C.).[1] Not only was Delphi despoiled of its treasures, which were unscrupulously seized by the Phocians, but Philip of Macedon was introduced as arbiter of the affairs of Hellas. Philip's entrance into the Hellenic world was a day of ruin for Greece in general, and for the Oracle in particular. Doubtless he meant well towards the Oracle and treated it with consideration. The same seems true of his son and successor, Alexander the Great, though that wayward monarch apparently showed but scant consideration for the time-honoured ritual forms.[2] Yet the Oracle soon perceived that it ceased to be the centre of attraction and that the " earth's centre " was transferred from Delphi to the Macedonian capital. It was shorn of all real liberty. With the power of Macedon dominating the world, Greek and Barbarian alike,

---

[1] For the Second Sacred War vid. Diod. xvi. 23 ff.; cf. Bury, " Hist. Gr." p. 695 ff.

[2] Cf. the story narrated in Plut. (Alex. xiv.) how Alexander came to consult the Oracle on one of the " nefast " days (ἀποφράδες ἡμέραι). The Pythia refused to give him a response, but he compelled her by force to sit upon the tripod. Under this constraint she declared, " my son, thou art invincible " (ἀνίκητος εἶ, ὦ παῖ); which words Alexander took to be an oracular utterance. The story, however, is of doubtful authenticity; we find practically the same said of Philomelus in Diod. xvi. 217: φθεξαμένης δὲ αὐτῆς . . . ὅτι ἔξεστιν αὐτῷ πράττειν ὃ βούλεται.

Decline and Fall of the Delphic Oracle

what wonder is it that the Oracle, too, sided with the conqueror? [1]

The Oracle, then, had fallen on evil days. Robbed of its treasures by the Phocians, it was robbed of its freedom by the Macedonians, its nominal champions. With the enslavement of Greece the Delphic shrine had lost that clientèle which of old had crowded from independent states to consult it on grave political questions. Its functions were now practically reduced to answering petty scruples or vulgar curiosities.[2] For more than a century after the rise of the Macedonian hegemony, the Oracle, bereft of political control, scarcely had any history. Kingdoms and dynasties were founded without its intervention. It had as protectors but the Macedonian kings, who, however, seem to have been more inclined to take than to give.[3] The resources of Greece had been wasted by long wars, and hence the Oracle had no chance of repairing that financial ruin which the Phocian usurpation

[1] Cf. Demosthenes' indignant exclamation, ἡ Πυθία φιλιππίζει (Plut. Dem. 20; Cic. De Div. ii. 57, § 118, "Demosthenes quidem, qui abhinc annos prope trecentos fuit, iam tum φιλιππίζειν Pythiam dicebat." Yet the Oracle is said to have predicted the death of Philip, vid. Diod. xvi. 91.

[2] Plut. (De Pyth. Orac. xxvi. xxviii.) contrasts the trivial questions of later times with the weighty consultations of the olden days: οὐδὲ γὰρ ὁ δεῖνα κατέβαινε μὰ Δία περὶ ὠνῆς ἀνδραπόδου χρησόμενος, οὐδὲ ὁ δεῖνα περὶ ἐργασίας· ἀλλὰ πόλεις μέγα δυνάμεναι καὶ βασιλεῖς καὶ τύραννοι, μέτριον οὐδὲν φρονοῦντες, ἐνετύγχανον τῷ θεῷ περὶ πραγμάτων.

[3] Cf. Bouché-Leclercq, op. cit. iii. pp. 190–1.

167

The Delphic Oracle

had wrought. It was inevitable that Delphi should share in the impoverishment of a decadent and depopulated Greece.[1] Faith, too, in the Oracle seems to have begun to wane appreciably, partly at least as a result of the rise and spread of philosophic scepticism ; so that to material ruin was added moral discredit. Hence we are not surprised that the temple which had been destroyed (probably by that frequent visitant, earthquake), about 371 B.C.,[2] was not rebuilt for more than half a century. What a contrast to the days of old ! There was now no munificent Croesus, or Gyges, or Gelon,[3] no Cnidians [4] with superabundant wealth, no generous Alcmaeonidae.[5] Thus the work was left to spasmodic efforts—and even these were largely on the part of the Peloponnesus—till eventually it was

[1] Vid. Plut. (De Def. Orac. viii. : . . . οὐδὲν οὖν ἕτερον ἦν τὸ πολλὰ καταλιπεῖν χρηστήρια τὸν θεὸν ἢ τῆς Ἑλλάδος ἐλέγχειν τὴν ἐρημίαν) on the failure of Greek oracles in general in later times. To the economic argument, however, Plut. adds a theosophical one—that the decline of oracles was due to the casual failing of "Demons" (ibid. xi. xv. xxxviii.), whom he regarded as the instruments of inspiration (ibid. xxxv. li.). Cf. Lucan, Phars v. 131–3, "muto Parnassus hiatu | conticuit, pressitque deum : seu spiritus istas | destituit fauces," etc.; Cic. De Div. ii. 57, § 117, " evanuisse aiunt vetustate vim loci eius, unde anhelitus ille terrae fieret, quo Pythia mente incitata oracula ederet."

[2] Vid. *B.C.H.* **xx.** p. 689.

[3] Vid. supr. p. 82, n. 1 and p. 93, n. 1.

[4] For the famous Treasury of the Cnidians (first wrongly assigned to the Siphnians) vid. Paus. x. 11. 2, 5 (with Frazer's " Comm."). Remains of it were discovered by the French excavators (vid. *B.C.H.* xx. pp. 581–602).

[5] Vid. supr. p. 85.

Decline and Fall of the Delphic Oracle

completed in the last quarter of the fourth century B.C.[1] Added to the Oracle's misfortunes was the fact that it was exposed to the attacks of an energetic and half-savage people, the Aetolians,[2] who had taken possession of Delphi, 290 B.C., and wished to take their place by force in the Pythian Amphictyony[3]—and all this with the practical consent of Hellas![4] There was now no Aeschines to rouse with his eloquence the Amphictyons against the sacrilegious usurpers. Nay, when some ten years later the ever-faithful Spartans asked for an effective muster against the Aetolians, they were suspected of aiming at the liberty of Greece![5]

Solitude was fast falling upon " the oracle of men," when in 279 B.C. a fortunate incident—fortunate at least in its issue—rescued it from ruin. The Gauls[6]—for centuries the menace of

[1] Vid. *B.C.H.* xx. p. 695. Cf. Delphic Paean to Dionysus, *B.C.H.* xix. p. 393 ff., where the poet (Philodamus of Scarphia) sighs for the completion of the temple.

[2] For the character of the Aetolians vid. Polyb. iv. 3. 1 : Αἰτωλοὶ . . . ἀεὶ πλεονεκτικὸν καὶ θηριώδη ζῶσι βίον, κ.τ.λ. ; cf. ibid. ii. 45. 1, etc.

[3] For the Aetolian usurpation vid. Just. xxiv. 1 ; Polyb. iv. 25. 8. Cf. Plut. Demetr. xl., who says that Demetrius Poliorcetes, king of Macedon, owing to the Aetolian occupation of Delphi, held the Pythian games at Athens.

[4] Cf. Just. l.c.

[5] Vid. Just. l.c. : " reparantibus deinde Spartanis bellum, auxilium multae civitates negaverunt, existimantes dominationem eos, non libertatem Graeciae, quaerere."

[6] For the Gallic invasion of Greece, 279 B.C. vid. Just. xxiv. 4-8 ; Paus. x. 19. 5-23. 14 ; Polyb. i. 6. 5, ii. 20. 6 ; 35. 7

The Delphic Oracle

Greece and Rome—under the leadership of " the Brennus " [1] had in the preceding year invaded Macedonia and defeated with great slaughter the forces of King Ptolemy Ceraunus. Having overrun all Macedonia the Gallic chieftain now turned his attention to the temples of the Immortals, mockingly remarking that " rich gods should be generous to men." From afar he pointed to the gleaming statues and chariots surmounting the terraces and temple façades, whetting the cupidity of his followers by declaring that these were constructed of solid gold.

National sentiment, however, revived before the barbarians. Phocians—eager doubtless to wipe out the former stain—Locrians and Aetolians rallied to the rescue of the sanctuary. Legend would have it, however, that the Oracle did not rely solely on human aid. " I and the white maidens shall take care of these matters " [2] said

and 9 ; iv. 16. 1, etc. ; Diod. xxii. 9. 5 ; Cic. De Div. i. 37, § 81.

[1] " Brennus " is very probably a title meaning " king " or " chieftain." Cf. Cymric *Brenhin*.

[2] Vid. Suidas, s.vv. ἐμοὶ μελήσει ταῦτα καὶ λευκαῖς κόραις. Cf. Cic. De Div. i. 37, § 81, " ego providebo rem istam et albae virgines." What exactly is meant by the " white maidens " is not clear. The reference, however, is probably to Artemis and Athene, vid. Just. xxiv. 8 : ". . . duas armatas virgines ex propinquis duabus Dianae Minervaeque aedibus," etc. The famous Apollo Belvedere is supposed to represent the god repelling the attack of the Gauls by shaking the aegis at them. With the expression ἐμοὶ μελήσει, κ.τ.λ., cf. Paus. x. 23. 1 : καὶ ὁ θεὸς οὐκ εἴα φοβεῖσθαι, φυλάξειν δὲ αὐτὸς ἐπηγγέλλετο τὰ ἑαυτοῦ. It

Decline and Fall of the Delphic Oracle

Apollo to the alarmed Delphians. The god was faithful to his word. For, with the Gallic onset, straightway from all the temples came priests and priestesses, wearing their insignia and with dishevelled hair, declaring that the god had come, and that they had seen him leap down into the temple through the opening in the roof-top ; that while they were suppliantly imploring aid of the god, a youth of superhuman size and surpassing beauty, accompanied by two virgins in armour from the neighbouring shrines of Artemis and Athene, had met them ; and not merely had they seen these : they had even heard the twanging of the bow and the clash of the armour.[1]

Thus encouraged, the gallant little band of defenders rushed to the fray, feeling, too, the divine intervention. A portion of the mountain suddenly torn away spread havoc among the assailants, while flashes of lightning blinded and consumed them. Heroes of the past, Hyperochus, Laodocus, Neoptolemus, Phylacus, mingled in the fray, repelling the barbarians.[2] The remnant of the Gauls perished in the ensuing night either by

is noteworthy that the narrative as given by Just. and Paus. agrees almost verbatim with that of Hdt. viii. 36–8, regarding the Persian attack on Delphi. Cf. also the account in Xen. Hell. vi. 4, 30, of the projected attack by Jason of Pherae upon the shrine : λέγεται δὲ ἐπερομένων τῶν Δελφῶν . . . ἀποκρίνασθαι τὸν θεὸν ὅτι αὐτῷ μελήσει.

[1] Vid. Just. xxiv. 8.
[2] Vid. Paus. i. 4. 4 ; x. 23. 2.

The Delphic Oracle

avalanches from Parnassus or by each other's hand. Such, according to tradition, was the end of the Gallic invasion of 279 B.C.

Yet these miracles do not seem to have prevented the pillaging of the shrine, as is probable enough from Livy,[1] Diodorus,[2] Appian[3] and the recently-discovered Delphic Hymn to Apollo.[4] Delivered, however, from the Gauls, the Greeks instituted the festival of Σωτήρια[5] in honour of Zeus Σωτήρ and Pythian Apollo. Celebrated every four years at Delphi, the games which constituted the festival included musical and poetical, as

---

[1] Vid. xxxviii. 48. 2 : "etiam Delphos quondam commune humani generis oraculum, umbilicum orbis terrarum, Galli spoliaverunt."

[2] Vid. i. 1 : Οὗτοι γάρ εἰσιν οἱ τὴν μὲν Ῥώμην ἑλόντες, τὸ δὲ ἱερὸν τὸ ἐν Δελφοῖς συλήσαντες.

[3] Vid. Illyr. v.: Τὴν Μακεδονίαν ἐπέδραμον ὁμοῦ καὶ τὴν Ἑλλάδα καὶ πολλὰ τῶν ἱερῶν καὶ τὸ Δελφικὸν ἐσύλησαν.

[4] Vid. B.C.H. xviii. p. 355, Hymn. Ap. 23-4. Polyb., however, repeatedly refers to the defeat of the Gauls on this occasion. Cf. i. 6. 5 : τῶν Γαλατῶν . . . τῶν τε περὶ Δελφοὺς φθαρέντων, κ.τ.λ. ; ii. 20. 6, etc. Yet he speaks of those Gauls "who had escaped the danger at Delphi" (διαφυγόντες τὸν περὶ Δελφοὺς κίνδυνον, vid. iv. 46. 1) as settling down near Byzantium, which they made tributary to them. Evidently, even according to Polyb., the army of "the Brennus".was far from being annihilated in the attack on Delphi, 279 B.C.

[5] The beginning of the decree, by which the Athenians associated themselves with the Aetolians in the institution of the festival, was discovered in 1860. Vid. Foucart, "Mém. sur Delph." p. 207. For a good account of this festival vid. Frazer, "Comm. Paus." x. 23. 13 ; Foucart, op. cit. pp. 207, 210-11 ; Mommsen, op. cit. p. 215 ff.

well as athletic and equestrian, contests, rivalling in splendour the Pythian games themselves.

But the attack of the Gauls had the effect of endowing the Oracle with renewed vitality—at least for a time. Yet that the old spirit was gone is clear enough from the tardiness with which the temple after its destruction was rebuilt, though indeed this was probably due in part to the general poverty of Greece. The remainder of the third century, however, and the whole of the second century B.C. seem to have been an epoch of comparative prosperity for the Oracle, as is shown by the numerous inscriptions for this period.[1]

The foreign relations of the Oracle during this epoch seem to have been happy. Attalus the First of Pergamum (241–197 B.C.) showed himself desirous of founding on the word of Apollo the legitimacy of his dynasty.[2] A decree was granted in honour of Eumenes the Second (197–159 B.C.), king of Pergamum, who had founded the games of Nicephoria and had invited the Delphians to send *theoroi*. The Aetolians, at this time masters of the Delphic sanctuary, manifested their gratitude by deciding that statues should be erected at Delphi to the king and his brothers.[3] We find also a decree of the Delphians in response to the

---

[1] Cf. *B.C.H.* xx. p. 703.

[2] Diod. Exc. Vatic. p. 105 ; Suidas, s.v. Ἄτταλος (quoted by Bouché-Leclercq, op. cit. iii. p. 191).

[3] Vid. *B.C.H.* xviii. p. 226 (quoting *B.C.H.* v. p. 376).

The Delphic Oracle

inhabitants of Sardis who having escaped great danger by the favour of the gods and the valour of king Eumenes the Second, had asked Delphi to recognize the founding of sacrifices, panegyrics, and new games on the occasion of their deliverance.[1] The Delphians instituted in honour of Attalus the Second (159–133 B.C.) festivals called 'Αττάλεια, and decreed a statue to him[2] in return for his generosity towards their shrine.

As it was with the kings of Pergamum, so also was it with the Seleucidae of Syria. From the reign of Seleucus the Second (246–226 B.C.) we have a decree of Delphi in answer to a letter of that king, asking for the sanctuary of Aphrodite Stratonicis and the town of Smyrna the privileges of being ἱερά and ἄσυλος. The Delphians granted the privilege.[3]

The same friendly relations were maintained between the Oracle and the Lagidae, kings of Egypt. In general those kings maintained Egyptian and Greek religion on an equal footing.[4] But there was one—most probably Ptolemy the Sixth (173–146 B.C.)—whose relations with Delphi were especially friendly. We read of his receiving deputations

[1] Vid. *B.C.H.* xviii. p. 226 (quoting *B.C.H.* v. p. 385).

[2] Ibid. (quoting *B.C.H.* v. p. 165).

[3] *B.C.H.* xviii. p. 230; vid. Tac. Ann. iii. 63, and inscr. of Smyrna (*C.I.G.* 3137), giving a treaty between Magnesia of Sipylus and Smyrna. Cf. the decree granting the privilege of ἀσυλία to the city of Antioch and the domain of Zeus Chrysorrhoas and Apollo, vid. *B.C.H.* xviii. p. 235.

[4] Ibid. p. 248.

Decline and Fall of the Delphic Oracle

from Delphic *theoroi*, who invite him to take part
in the festival of " Soteria." [1] Similar are the relations of the Delphic sanctuary with the kingdom
of Bithynia from the third to the first century B.C.
We have a decree of Delphi in honour of king
Nicomedes and queen Laodice, daughter of Mithri-
dates. The Nicomedes here mentioned is Nicomedes
the Third (91–74 B.C.).[2]

But with the beginning of the first century B.C.
silence again falls upon the Delphic sanctuary.[3]
We find no more mention of feasts, no catalogues
of Athenian *theoriai*, no lists of Dionysiac artists
(both so common in the third and second centuries
B.C.) after 97 B.C.[4] Scarcely at long intervals is
the name of Delphi mentioned, and even then not
always to its credit.[5] For the first time, after the
battle of Philippi, 42 B.C., the state of Delphi received benevolent attention. Mark Antony declared his intention of repairing the temple,[6] which
once more had been destroyed by fire, 83 B.C.[7]
The project, however, was not completed. Augustus,

[1] *B.C.H.* xviii. p. 248.
[2] Ibid. p. 254.   [3] Vid. *B.C.H.* xviii. p. 786.
[4] *B.C.H.* xviii. (Homolle), p. 706.
[5] Cic. De Div. ii. 117, says of it " . . . iam ut nihil possit
esse contemptius." Vid. supr. p. 64, n. 1. In history Delphi is
mentioned as occupied by Fufius Calenus in the name of Caesar
(vid. Caes. Civ. Bell. iii. 55. 4).
[6] Plut. Ant. 23: Πρὸς δὲ καὶ τὸν τοῦ Πυθίου νεὼν κατεμέτρησεν
ὡς συντελέσων· τοῦτο γὰρ ὑπέσχετο πρὸς τὴν σύγκλητον.
[7] *B.C.H.* xx. p. 703.

The Delphic Oracle

who had reorganized the Amphictyonic Council [1] and had everywhere revived the ancient cults, could not absolutely neglect the temple. Plutarch [2] tells us that the empress Livia dedicated an E in gold to replace the old mysterious letter of bronze or of wood.

SECTION B : ATTEMPTED REVIVAL OF THE DELPHIC ORACLE

Such was the plight of the Oracle towards the end of the first century B.C. Nevertheless, at the beginning of the Christian era we notice some symptoms of a revival. The Athenians reappear regularly at the temple ; enfranchisements are revived ; but still the practical abandonment of the Oracle persists. Nero's attitude towards it is rather difficult to understand. Now we are told that he completed the new temple (always interrupted) during his visit to Greece (66–7),[3] now that he

---

[1] Paus. x. 8. 3.

[2] De E apud Delph. iii. (τὸ μὲν χρυσοῦν E Λιβίας τῆς Καίσαρος γυναικός). Vid. supr. p. 142.

[3] Vid. Schol. Aeschin. In Ctesiph. 116, who, however, cites no authorities. According to Koehler, the scholiast misinterpreted ἐξειργάσθαι (or ἐξεργάσασθαι), the reference being not to material completion, but to the performance of some religious ceremony. Yet the author of the Prolegomena to the rhetor Aristides says that Nero built a structure larger and more beautiful than the old one, and afterwards destroyed it because a response was given to a poor peasant, which was refused to himself. Vid. B.C.H. xx. p. 710.

Decline and Fall of the Delphic Oracle

gave the Pythia 100,000 denarii for prophesying as
he wished, yet afterwards took away from the
temple the Cirrhaean lands and distributed them
among his soldiers, and finally choked the fissure
of inspiration with corpses.[1] Pseudo-Lucian refers
merely to the Oracle's freedom of speech which made
Nero set about stopping the oracular chasm.[2]
Pausanias [3] refers to nothing but the removal of 500
statues from the sanctuary. More significant still
is the silence of Plutarch, who was at Delphi at the
time, and who mentions Nero's visit.[4] Yet he
makes no reference to any act of violence on the
part of Nero. It would seem, then, that the stories
of his violence towards the Oracle are either entirely
or largely inventions. His conduct on the whole
was most probably beneficent. At least that a
policy of public attention to the Oracle on the part
of the Romans was initiated by Nero seems to be
the inference from the benevolent interest shown
by the Flavian emperors. Vespasian had regulated
certain financial questions and territory interesting
the Delphians.[5] Titus was honorary archon at
Delphi, A.D. 79.[6] We find in Delphic inscriptions
repeated marks of interest on the part of Domitian

[1] Dio Cass. lxiii. 14 (quoted by Homolle, *B.C H*. xx. p. 710).
[2] Nero, x.: . . . καὶ γὰρ δὴ τὸ Πυθικὸν στόμιον παρ' οὗ αἱ ὀμφαὶ
ἀνέπνεον ἀποφράττειν ὥρμησεν, ὡς μηδὲ τῷ Ἀπόλλωνι φωνὴ εἴη.
Allusion to the murder of Agrippina was the cause of Nero's
anger.
[3] x. 7. 1.   [4] Vid. De E apud Delph. i.
[5] *B.C.H*. xx. (Homolle), p. 712.   [6] *B.C.H*. xviii. p. 97.

The Delphic Oracle

for the town of Delphi, its privileges and feasts. An inscription—discovered in fragments by the French—shows that the temple was repaired by Domitian in A.D. 84.[1] The enterprise indicates the new favour which the temple of Delphi and the cult of Apollo began to enjoy at this period from thinkers and politicians. It was simply an attempt, political and intellectual, at the revival of paganism[2] in opposition to the spread of Christianity. It is noteworthy that the first persecutors of Christians, Nero and Domitian, were also restorers of the Apolline sanctuary. When the temple is repaired, we find the Pythian games restored, the town of Delphi enlarged and embellished, philosophers, sophists, etc., flocking to Delphi and sojourning there.[3] Of the revival Plutarch is the best representative.

The same policy was continued under Nerva, Trajan and Hadrian. Hadrian was himself twice honorary archon.[4] Especially under the reigns of

[1] Vid. *B.C.H.* xx. p. 717. The inscr. (as emended and restored) reads thus :

Imp(erator) [Caesa]r D(ivi Ves)pa[sia]ni [f. Do]mitianu[s] Aug. [Germa]nic[us pont. max]im. [trib. potest.] III, p.p.imp. VII, cos X d[es XI, templum] Ap[ollinis sua i]npensa refecit.

[2] For this revival vid. Plut. De Pyth. Orac. xxix.

[3] *B.C.H.* xx. p. 715, vid. supr. p. 76.

[4] Hadrian consulted the Oracle in person regarding the birthplace of Homer. The response of the Pythia made out the poet to be " an immortal siren," and grandson of Nestor and Odysseus. Vid. Anth. Pal. xiv. 102 : ἄγνωστον μ' ἐρέεις γενεῆς καὶ πατρίδος αἴης | ἀμβροσίου Σειρῆνος, κ.τ.λ.

Decline and Fall of the Delphic Oracle

Trajan and Hadrian do we find the cult of Apollo fostered by a series of legislative documents.[1] Hadrian reorganized the Amphictyonic Council, and regulated the question of the administration of finance and the games.[2] The new period of prosperity had now reached its climax : Delphi was become as of old " the Sacred City " (ἁ ἱερὰ πόλις).

But this religious reform had too forced a character. It was too much the work of savants to take a firm hold upon the populace and thereby have an abiding effect. And so, after the Antonines and Severus [3] silence falls anew upon the Delphic sanctuary. The decline is this time decisive. Only at long intervals is the Oracle's existence shown by a few inscriptions in honour of emperors, graven poorly on poor materials.[4] There is no longer any reference to the temple even in literature. The physical ruin of the temple is already taking place for the

---

[1] We have a record of judgments given in the name of Trajan by his legate Avidius Nigrinus. Vid. the famous bilingual document (discovered and published by Wescher) referring to litigations about frontiers which had been going on for centuries between Delphi and the neighbouring cities of Amphissa, Myonia, Anticyra and Ambrysus (*B.C.H.* xx. p. 719).

[2] Vid. *P.W.* (s.v. Delphoi), 2581.

[3] For a statue dedicated to Severus at Delphi vid. *B.C.H.* vi. p. 453. According to Spartianus (Pescenn. Niger) the Oracle had predicted to Severus his future, and the fall of his rivals. The Delphians remained faithful to Severus and his son. Under the dynasty of the Severi for the last time Delphic epigraphy mentions the temple (vid. *B.C.H.* xx. p. 727).

[4] Vid. *B.C.H.* xx. p. 728. The French excavators found the base of a statue dedicated to Valerian.

The Delphic Oracle

embellishment of Constantinople : [1] its moral ruin
is effected by Christianity, which now has triumphed
over all obstacles, and has hoisted the standard of
Christ upon the Capitol.

Julian attempted the revival of paganism, but
his efforts were fruitless.[2] The Oracle broke its
silence only to proclaim to the emperor its down-
fall. " Tell the king," said the Pythia, " to earth
is fallen the deft-wrought dwelling, no longer hath
Phoebus shelter, or prophetic laurel, or speaking
fountain ; yea, the speaking water is quenched." [3]
Such was the last utterance that broke from the
Delphic shrine, such the last whisper of desolation,
the death-song of the Pythian prophetess. Theo-
dosius took the Oracle at its word, and had the
temple closed ; [4] Arcadius, his successor, demolished

---

[1] Vid. *B.C.H.* xx. p. 715 ; *P.W.* l.c. 2583.

[2] Vid. *B.C.H.* xx. p. 730 ; *P.W.* l.c. 2582-3. Julian granted
the impoverished Delphians exemption from taxes, vid.
Julian, Epist. 35 (quoted by Bouché-Leclercq, op. cit. III.
p. 206).

[3] εἴπατε τῷ βασιλῆϊ· χαμαὶ πέσε δαίδαλος αὐλά | οὐκέτι Φοῖβος ἔχει
καλύβαν, οὐ μάντιδα δάφναν, | οὐ παγὰν λαλέουσαν· ἀπέσβετο καὶ λάλον
ὕδωρ. Vid. *P.W.* l.c. 2583 (quoting from Cedren. Hist. Comp.
i. 304). The response was delivered, it was said, to Julian's
quaestor and physician, Oribasius, who consulted the Oracle on
behalf of the emperor when departing on his expedition against
Persia, A.D. 362. The response, however, is of somewhat doubtful authenticity : according to Eusebius (vid. *B.C.H.* xx.
p. 709) it was addressed to Augustus. With the expression
ἀπέσβετο καὶ λάλον ὕδωρ cf. σεσίγηται γοῦν ἡ Κασταλίας πηγή, κ.τ.λ.
(Euseb. Pr. Ev. ii. 3. 2, quoting Clem. Alex. Protrept.).

[4] Circ. A.D. 390.

Decline and Fall of the Delphic Oracle

it.[1]   The Delphic Oracle is fallen—fallen to rise no
more. . . .

> " Apollo from his shrine
> Can no more divine,
> With hollow shriek the steep of Delphos leaving."[2]

---

[1] The temple was not protected as in many cases by being
consecrated to Christian worship, though much of the marble
of the various edifices was employed in the decoration of Christian churches, as well as in the adornment of Constantinople.
Everywhere there are indications not of transformation but of
destruction.   What the Christians, anxious to wipe out all
traces of paganism, left undone, was completed by the ravages
of nature : such destruction could have been effected only by
violent upheavals.   (Vid. *B.C.H.* xx. pp. 729–32.)

As early as the sixth cent. Christianity was installed at Delphi.
The French excavators found a Christian epitaph which must
apparently be assigned to the sixth cent. containing the name
of a bishop named Pantamianos.

[2] Milton, " Hymn on the Nativity," 176–8.

APPENDIX A

THE PYTHON

THE Python designates the dragon slain by Apollo, the *locus classicus* for which episode is the Homeric Hymn.[1] As to the name, the dragon in the Homeric

---

[1] Vid. Hom. Hymn. Ap. 300–4, 356–70. The combat of the dragon at Delphi with Apollo was celebrated by what was known as the " Pythian Strain " (Νόμος Πυθικός). Vid. Pollux, iv. 84: δήλωμα δ' ἐστι ὁ νόμος τῆς τοῦ Ἀπόλλωνος μάχης πρὸς τὸν δράκοντα. The chief item in the musical programme at the Pythian games, the " Pythian Strain," had for its composer Sacadas of Argos. Vid. Paus. ii. 22. 8 : τὸ αὔλημα τὸ Πυθικὸν πρῶτος (sc. Σακάδας) ηὔλησεν ἐν Δελφοῖς ; Pollux, iv. 78 : ὁ δὲ Σακάδα νόμος Πυθικός. It was in the main a flute-solo, but that other instruments, such as the lyre and trumpet, were used (at least in certain parts) is the obvious inference from Strab. (p. 421) : προσέθεσαν δὲ τοῖς κιθαρῳδοῖς αὐλητάς τε καὶ κιθαριστάς, κ.τ.λ. Cf. Pollux (iv. 84) : . . . τὰ σαλπιστικὰ κρούματα. Pollux (iv. 84) distinguishes five parts : πεῖρα, κατακελευσμός, ἰαμβικὸν, σπονδεῖον, καταχόρευσις. The first (πεῖρα) described the god's reconnoitring the battle-ground, the second (κατακελευσμός) his challenge to the dragon ; the third (ἰαμβικόν)—in which the trumpet-blasts (σαλπιστικὰ κρούματα) represented the twanging of Apollo's bow and the whizzing of his arrows, while the strains of the flute imitated now the gnashing of the dragon's teeth (ὀδοντισμός), now the hissing of his dying breath (συριγμός)—described the actual combat. The fourth part (σπονδεῖον) described the decision of the victory for the god, the fifth (καταχόρευσις) represented the god's triumphal dance. Strabo (p. 421) also enumerates five parts, which, however, are somewhat different : πέντε δ' αὐτοῦ μέρη

Appendix A

Hymn is nameless : it is simply δράκαινα.[1] So, too, in Euripides[2] and Pausanias[3] it is still nameless, though the gender has changed to the male (δράκων). The change in gender has been explained as due to a desire to provide a worthier foe for Apollo.[4] In later times, however, when a name was given to the dragon the same confusion of gender continues. The most usual name was Πυθών, a name found for the first time in Strabo (quoting from the euhemerist Ephorus).[5] Other names were Δελφύνη or Δελφύνης, given by the Alexandrine School.[6] The name Πυθών was evidently derived in the same way as Πυθώ was derived by the writer of the Homeric Hymn to Apollo—from πύθεσθαι, " rot,"[7] because the dragon slain by Apollo there rotted.

ἐστίν, ἄγκρουσις, ἄμπειρα, κατακελευσμός, ἴαμβοι καὶ δάκτυλοι, σύριγγες. The ἄγκρουσις he explains as an overture or prelude to the piece : ἄγκρουσιν μὲν τὸ προοίμιον δηλῶν. For the parts of the Νόμος Πυθικός vid. also Schol. Hypoth. Pind. P. p. 297 (Boeckh). For a good treatment of the question vid. Mommsen, " Delphika," pp. 175, 177, 183, 193–4 ; Schreiber, " Apollon Pythoktonos," p. 22 ff.

[1] Cf. l. 300: ἔνθα δράκαιναν κτεῖνεν, ἄναξ Διὸς υἱός. So, too, St. George was said to have killed a nameless dragon or " worm." For the prevalence of dragon-slaying feats in " Aryan " myth —and even outside it, e.g. in Japanese myth—vid. " The Celtic Dragon-Myth," by J. F. Campbell, pp. xviii, xxiv, etc.

[2] I. T. 1245: οἰνωπὸς δράκων.

[3] x. 6. 5.   [4] Miss Harrison in *J.H.S.* xix. p. 222 f.

[5] 422. 12. Cf. Apollod. Bibl. i. 43 (quoted by Farnell, op. cit. iv. p. 383).

[6] Vid. Bouché-Leclercq, op. cit. iii. p. 56.

[7] For this derivation of Πυθώ from πύθεσθαι, " rot," vid. Hom. Hymn. Ap. 371–2 ; Paus. x. 6. 5, who vouches that this was the common derivation in ancient times. Cf. supr. p. 1, n. 1.

The Python

What was the Python ? In the account of Apollo's victory given by the writer of the Homeric Hymn, the victim of Apollo's wrath is simply a she-dragon (δράκαινα), "a fell monster," having its abode near a "fair-flowing fountain."[1] Pausanias[2] is more explicit, saying that the dragon slain by Apollo was set by Earth as a guardian of her shrine. This idea that the dragon was the guardian of the Earth-shrine is borne out by Euripides,[3] the writers of two hymns recently discovered at Delphi,[4] Aelian,[5] and Apollodorus.[6]

But in the fragment of old Delphic oracular verse quoted by Pausanias,[7] he whom Apollo slew was

---

[1] Vid. 1. 300. The fountain in question is generally regarded as the Castalian spring. But Frazer identifies it with the spring called Cassotis by Paus. (x. 24. 7). For the probable dwelling of the Python vid. supr. p. 4, n. 7 ; Frazer, "Comm. Paus." ix. 10. 5 ; x. 12. 1; cf. Eur. Phoen. 232: ζάθεα τ' ἄντρα δράκοντος. For the idea of a dragon guarding a well vid. Paus. ix. 10. 5, and numerous examples given by Frazer ("Comm." on passage) of similar beliefs among various peoples.

[2] x. 6. 3.

[3] I. T. 1247–8 : . . . ποικιλόνωτὸς οἰνωπὸς δράκων ἀμφέπε μαντεῖον χθόνιον.

[4] Cf. Hymn. Ap. (B.C.H. xvii. p. 574 and xviii. PL. xxv ; Otto Crusius, "Die Delph. Hymnen," Phil. '94, p. 30 ff.), l. 19: [τρ]ίποδα μαντεῖον ὡς εἷλες ἐχθρὸς ὃν ἐφρούρει δράκων ; Second Hymn to Ap. (B.C.H. xviii. p. 345), l. 28, where Python is said to be the " child of Earth ": [τ]ὸμ παῖδα Γᾶ[ας] τ' ἔπεφνες ἰοῖς. Cf. Plut. De Pyth. Orac. xxvii., " Earth's crafty son, the dragon " (Γῆς τε δράκοντα δόλιον υἱόν), and Hdt. i. 78.

[5] Var. Hist. iii. 1.

[6] Bibl. 1. 4: ὡς ὁ φρουρῶν τὸ μαντεῖον Πυθὼν ὄφις, κ.τ.λ.

[7] x. 6. 7: . . . σίντῃ Παρνήσοιο. Cf. the legend given by Paus. (ibid.) that he who was slain by Ap. was the " overbearing son of Crius, a chieftain of Euboea, who rifled the sanc-

Appendix A

" a robber of Parnassus," for whose slaying Apollo
had to be " purified by Cretan men." Strabo [1]
(quoting Ephorus) gives a euhemerist version that
Python was a " cruel man " (χαλεπὸν ἄνδρα) sur-
named "Dragon " (Δράκων), who infested Parnassus,
but, like Tityus at Panopeae, was slain by the " far-
darting " god. In Hyginus [2] we find the legend
that before the days of Apollo the Python was
wont to give oracles on Mount Parnassus. We find
a somewhat similar statement made by the Scholiast
in the Argument to the Pythian Odes of Pindar.[3]

We may take it that the dragon at Delphi represents an earlier cult, conquered and dispossessed
by Apollo—most probably the cult of Ge. For this
we have proof in the legends already mentioned
which represent the dragon Python as the protector
or interpreter, or even the offspring, of Earth. The
snake at Delphi most probably was the symbol, or
embodiment, of the Earth-divinity. We have other
instances of a similar association, notably in the
case of the famous snake-goddess of Gournia,
where a goddess, who is almost certainly an Earth-
divinity, is represented as twined round with
snakes.[4]

But how do we explain such association of the
snake with the Earth-goddess at Delphi ? The
tuary of the god and the houses of wealthy men " ; Plut. (De
Def. Orac. xv.) seems inclined to a view of this kind.

[1] 422. 12.

[2] Fab. 140 (quoted by Farnell, op. cit. iv. p. 382), " Python
ante Apollinem ex oraculo in monte Parnasso responsa dare solitus
est. . . ." Cf. Clem. Alex. Protr. 29: Πυθοῖ ὁ δράκων θρησκεύεται.

[3] Πυθῶνος δὲ τότε κυριεύσαντος τοῦ προφητικοῦ τρίποδος.

[4] Vid. R. M. Burrows, " Cretan Discoveries," p. 27 ; cf. also
Farnell, op. cit. iii. pp. 295-6.

The Python

snake was a mystic or sacred animal in Greek religion. It was constantly throughout Greece associated with the chthonic divinities,[1] and was frequently regarded as possessing mantic powers.[2] It was often considered the incarnation of a departed spirit. Heroes were commonly represented by snakes. Frequently we find on vase-paintings snakes depicted on the very grave-mound itself.[3]

The snake, then, was so constantly associated with the chthonic powers that we need not be sur-

---

[1] Cf. the feast of the Thesmophoria, held in honour of Δημήτηρ Θεσμοφόρος, where μιμήματα δρακόντων (" images of snakes ") were used; vid. Farnell, op. cit. iii. p. 327 (quoting Lucian, Hetaer.) ; cf. Miss Harrison, " Proleg." p. 121. Cf. also the shrine of Trophonius at Lebadaea, where there was a prophetic snake, which had to be propitiated with offerings of honey cakes (μάζας μεμαγμένας μέλιτι, Paus. ix. 39. 11). It is highly probable that Ge herself was one of the aboriginal powers of the Trophonium, but was supplanted by her double, the nymph Hercyna, whose emblem was the snake (cf. Farnell, op. cit. iii. p. 10). Cf. also the Italian *genius loci*, a fertility daimon, who was constantly represented by a snake. (Vid. picture found at Herculaneum, reproduced in Smith's " Class. Dict." s.v. Genius).

[2] For other instances of oracular snakes besides that of Delphi vid. Paus. ix. 39. 11 (oracle of Troph. just mentioned) ; cf. also the shrines of Asclepius where tame serpents were supposed to whisper cures " into the ears " of consultants during sleep (vid. Farnell, op. cit. iii. p. 10). According to Ael. Nat. An. ii. 2 (quoted by Farnell, op. cit. iv. p. 402) there was in Epirus a system of divination by means of tame serpents. The statement of Aelian, then, ἴδιον ἦν τῶν δρακόντων καὶ ἡ μαντική, seems justified.

[3] Cf. the altar to a hero found in Lesbos with inscr. " the people to Aristandrus, the hero." Snakes are sculptured round the cup for receiving libations, vid. Miss Harrison, " Proleg." p. 325.

Appendix A

prised at the association of the Python or dragon with the Earth-goddess of Delphi. Hence we conclude that the famous story of the conflict between Apollo and the Python represents an important event in the religious history of Delphi—a conflict of the chthonian with the Apolline cult. The old theory [1] that it represents an atmospheric conflict of sunshine, storm, and thunder-cloud, that the slaying of the dragon symbolizes the driving away of winter and darkness by the return of spring and light, is now generally discarded.

---

[1] For the old theory vid. Bouché-Leclercq, op. cit. iii. p. 63 ; Foucart, "Mém. sur Delph." pp. 131–2. As has been already pointed out, this dragon-slaying prevails largely throughout "Aryan" myth. Certainly some forms of it—for which vid. J. F. Campbell's "Celtic Dragon-Myth"—are strangely reminiscent of the Python-legend of Delphi. As to the origin of these myths it is difficult to say for certain how far they have been transmitted from one people to another. Certainly some of them are pure nature-myths, e.g. the struggle of Indra and Ahi in the Rig Veda. Here the combat represents the triumph of sunshine over cloud, of light over darkness.

APPENDIX B

THE HOSII

WHO were those Hosii (Ὅσιοι), the "holy ones" of Delphi? They are mentioned only by Plutarch,[1] who says that they were five in number, chosen from the most ancient families of Delphi, and holding office for life. They claimed descent from Deucalion (the Noah of Greek mythology). Were they identical with, or distinct from, the priests (ἱερεῖς)? Apparently they were distinct—though so great an authority as Dr. Farnell seems to regard them as identical; for he constantly speaks of the "holy ones" (Ὅσιοι), to whom he attributes the direction of affairs generally at Delphi. That they were distinct from the priests is the probable inference from the statement of Plutarch:[2] οἱ γὰρ ἱερεῖς κ α ì Ὅσιοι θύειν φασὶ τὸ ἱερεῖον, κ.τ.λ., "for the priests *and* the 'holy ones' say that they offer up the victim," etc. Here the conjunction seems to show that they were distinct bodies. Again, the προφῆται,[3] "prophets" (for there were more

---

[1] Quaest. Gr. ix.: πέντε δέ εἰσιν Ὅσιοι διὰ βίου, καὶ τὰ πολλὰ μετὰ τῶν προφητῶν δρῶσιν οὗτοι, καὶ συνιερουργοῦσιν ἅτε γεγονέναι δοκοῦντες ἀπὸ Δευκαλίωνος.

[2] De Def. Orac. xlix.

[3] These "prophets," i.e. interpreters, were chosen by lot from among noble Delphian families (Eur. Ion, 416: Δελφῶν ἀριστῆς, οὓς ἐκλήρωσε πάλος). Their function was to interpret, i.e. put in

Appendix B

than one προφήτης), were identical with the priests, as is shown by the fact that in Plutarch in one passage Nicander is called προφήτης,[1] while in another he is called ἱερεύς.[2] But the prophets and Hosii were distinct, as is clear enough from Plutarch.[3] Therefore, we conclude that the priests and the Hosii were distinct.

Who, then, were the Hosii, and what were their functions ? Various views have been put forward.

(*a*) Bouché-Leclercq regards them as the remnant of an anterior priesthood analogous to the Selloi of Dodona.[4] But, as in the case of so many of his statements, he fails to give any ground for his theory.

intelligible form—usually in (hexameter) verse—the cries of the Pythia under inspiration. Apparently only one " prophet" acted at a time, cf. Plut. De Def. Orac. li. The response was always thought to be dictated by the Pythia, who spoke in the first person, as representing the god himself. But according to Plutarch (De Pyth. Orac. xxv.) it was always suspected that the poetic composition did not come from the god—and no wonder, for its quality was usually not the best. For Iambic responses vid. Hdt. i. 74 ; Paus. iv. 9. 4, and the famous χρησμός about Socrates. For responses in *prose* vid. Plut. De Pyth. Orac. xxiii. ff. ; Strab. 419. 6 ; Cic. De Div. ii. 57, § 116, " praeterea Pyrrhi temporibus iam Apollo versus facere desierat."

[1] De Def. Orac. li.   [2] De E apud Delph. v.

[3] De Def. Orac. li.: . . . ὥστε φυγεῖν μὴ μόνον τοὺς θεοπρόπους, ἀλλὰ καὶ τὸν προφήτην Νίκανδρον καὶ τοὺς παρόντας τῶν Ὁσίων, . . . " so that not only the consulters took to flight, but even the interpreter Nicander, *and* such of the Holy Ones as were present." The last conjunction seems to show that the " prophet " was distinct from the " Holy Ones."

[4] Op. cit. iii. pp. 50, 94, " . . . les débris d'un sacerdoce antérieur analogue à la corporation des Selloi de Dodone."

The Hosii

(*b*) A. Mommsen [1] supposes that the Hosii preserved at Delphi the archaic cult of Prometheus.
As grounds for his statement he adduces the fact
that Deucalion, from whom the Hosii claimed descent, was regarded as the son of Prometheus, and
also the fact that at Panopeus on Mount Parnassus
north of Delphi was shown the clay out of which
Prometheus created man. [2] But if the Hosii were
priests of Prometheus, why should they offer sacrifice to Dionysus ? How, furthermore, do we explain their importance at Delphi ?

(*c*) Miss Harrison regards them as Dionysiac. [3]
The grounds which she gives for her theory are,
first, that they claimed descent from Deucalion,
who marks Thessalian ancestry and Thessaly looks
North, from which Dionysus came (a not too
cogent reason certainly !) ; secondly, that the words
῞Οσιος and Ὁσιωτήρ [4] are particularly Dionysiac ;
thirdly, that according to Plutarch " the Hosii
offer secret sacrifice in the sanctuary of Apollo,
when the Thyiads waken him of the winnowing-
fan " (Λικνίτης). [5]
This last view seems the most probable. That
they were Dionysiac is perhaps borne out by the
statement of Plutarch that " these (i.e. the Hosii)
perform most duties along with the prophets." [6]
This is just what we should expect in later times,

1 " Delphika," pp. 256–7.   2 Vid. Paus. x. 4. 3.

3 " Prolegomena," p. 500 ff.

4 Ὁσιωτήρ was the name of the victim, when one of the Hosii
was appointed (Plut. Quaest. Gr. ix.).

5 Plut. De Is. et Os. xxxv.: καὶ θύουσιν οἱ ῞Οσιοι ἀπόρρητον ἐν τῷ
ἱερῷ τοῦ Ἀπόλλωνος, ὅταν αἱ Θυιάδες ἐγείρωσι τὸν Λικνίτην.

6 Plut. Quaest. Gr. ix., vid. supr. p. 189, n. 1.

Appendix B

when, as we have seen, Dionysus came to be the cult-brother of Apollo at Delphi.[1] But what of their claim to be descended from Deucalion and the fact that they were drawn from the oldest families in Delphi? For, was not Dionysus a comparatively late comer to Delphi?[2] We may answer, perhaps, that this claim was a latter-day exaggeration on the part of the Hosii, due to an attempt to heighten their own prestige by boasting of an ancient lineage. We have a similar exaggeration in the statement (already referred to) that Dionysus was the first to give oracles at Delphi.[3] It seems most likely, then, that the "holy ones" of Delphi were none other than priests of the son of Semele.

[1] Vid. supr. pp. 33-4, 117.   [2] Vid. supr. pp. 30-2.
[3] Vid. supr. p. 31.

INDEX

Index

Index

Index

196

Index

197

Index

Index

Index